JERRY D. THOMAS

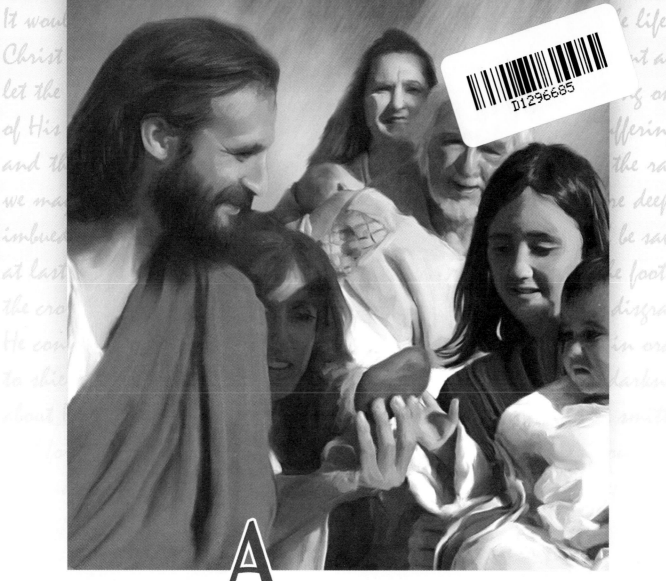

A THOUGHTFUL HOUR 2

Living the Beatitudes

Pacific Press®
Publishing Association

Nampa, Idaho | Oshawa, Ontario, Canada
www.pacificpress.com

Cover design by Gerald Lee Monks
Cover resources from Sermon View
Inside design by Kristin Hansen-Mellish

The author assumes full responsibility for the accuracy of all facts and quotations as cited in this book.

Unless otherwise noted, Scripture quotations are from the King James Version of the Bible.

GOD'S WORD is a copyrighted work of God's Word to the Nations. Quotations are used by permission. Copyright © 1995 by God's Word to the Nations. All rights reserved.

Scripture quotations marked NASB are taken from the NEW AMERICAN STANDARD BIBLE®, Copyright © 1960, 1962, 1963, 1968, 1971, 1972, 1973, 1975, 1977, 1995 by The Lockman Foundation. Used by permission.

Scriptures marked NCV are taken from the New Century Version®. Copyright © 2005 by Thomas Nelson, Inc. Used by permission. All rights reserved.

Scripture quotations marked NIV are from the HOLY BIBLE, NEW INTERNATIONAL VERSION®. Copyright © 1973, 1978, 1984, 2011 by Biblica, Inc.® Used by permission. All rights reserved worldwide. This book uses the 1984 edition.

You can obtain additional copies of this book by calling toll-free 1-800-765-6955 or by visiting http://www.adventistbookcenter.com.

ISBN 978-0-8163-6146-5

February 2016

A THOUGHTFUL HOUR 2

Also by Jerry D. Thomas

Dedication

To all of us who would have
. . . stepped along the lake through the darkness,
. . . climbed the paths along the hillside,
. . . held hope in our hearts that a new day was truly dawning.

Who wish they could have been there that morning with Jesus.

Contents

Foreword

The psalmist David, perhaps the foremost devotional expositor in Scripture, writes the following in Psalm 16:11: "You will make known to me the path of life; in Your presence is fullness of joy; in Your right hand there are pleasures forever" (NASB). This brief meditation is but one of the gems hidden in Psalm 16—a piece of wisdom literature not to be missed. Here David expresses complete joy in the presence of God—a joy born of total surrender to the will of God. And what are the benefits of time spent in God's presence, says he? Fullness of joy and pleasures forever! Surely these blessings are worth our time, are they not?

While David's beautiful meditation encourages us to submit our lives to the invigorating rays of the Divine, day-to-day life seems to conspire against this noble endeavor. We have jobs to do, bills to pay, places to go, people to see, and media to enjoy. Technologies that promised to save us time have done the opposite, leaving us more busy and bothered than ever before. Like the proverbial rat on the wheel, we run faster and faster with no destination in sight.

Ellen White, another inspired devotional enthusiast, understood keenly the promise of time spent with God. In *The Desire of Ages* she even goes so far as to suggest a Subject worthy of our time and thought. "It would be well," she wrote, "for us to spend a thoughtful hour in contemplation of the life of Christ" (page 83). This book is designed to help you get the most out of time spent reflecting on the life of Christ.

As you prepare to unearth treasures hidden in the life and ministry of Jesus, know that when you do this, you will be following in the footsteps of Christ Himself. He allowed no earthly duty to supersede the supreme calling to spend time with His Father. Luke writes in his Gospel, "Jesus Himself would often slip away to the wilderness and pray" (Luke 5:16, NASB). In the presence of His Father, Jesus received direction, affirmation, and strength for the journey. No wonder He could say to the disciples, "He who sent Me is with Me; He has not left Me alone, for I always do the things that are pleasing to Him" (John 8:29, NASB). If Jesus craved the presence of God, shouldn't we?

As you contemplate the life of Christ, you will find purpose for your existence, passion for your purpose, and power to live that purpose every day.

Dwain N. Esmond
Associate Director
The Ellen G. White Estate, Inc.

Introduction

"It would be well for us to spend a thoughtful hour each day in contemplation of the life of Christ."
—*The Desire of Ages*, 83

"Let us in imagination go back to that scene, and, as we sit with the disciples on the mountainside, enter into the thoughts and feelings that filled their hearts. Understanding what the words of Jesus meant to those who heard them, we may discern in them a new vividness and beauty, and may also gather for ourselves their deeper lessons."
—*Thoughts From the Mount of Blessing*, 1

Not long ago, I stood on the shore of the Sea of Galilee at the break of dawn. From where I stood, I could hear the wavelets rustling the rocks along the water's edge. I could see the reeds bending back and forth in their endless dance with the water. I could see the reflection of the breaking dawn on the lake as it might have looked that morning long ago when Jesus sat before a crowd of people and shared some of the most precious words of Scripture.

From where I stood, I looked across the lake as the sun began to light up the tops of the hills around Capernaum. Somewhere, surely within my gaze, was the spot where Jesus had led the crowd and sat to share what we call the Sermon on the Mount.

In spite of the language we know from the King James Version, the Sea of Galilee is not a sea. It's a large freshwater lake, beautiful and blue in the morning light. And the hills around the lake are not mountains, so the Sermon on the Hillside would be more accurate. Yet in the early morning light, it is a beautiful sight.

As I stood there, I tried to imagine what it would have been like to have been there that morning. Waking up before dawn to find my way to the lake to see Jesus, or perhaps sleeping on the ground near the lake knowing that Jesus was somewhere nearby. Would I be hoping to see someone healed? Was I wishing that Jesus would feed us all with fish and bread? Was I hoping to be on the front lines if Jesus declared Himself King and asked for volunteers for His army?

Putting ourselves on the scene that day will help us hear the words of Jesus more clearly and understand what they should mean in our lives today. But to do this, we have to take time each day—perhaps a thoughtful hour—reading and studying His words.

As precious as the story of Jesus is to each of us, our daily lives keep us so busy that it's hard to carve out the time we would like to spend learning about Him. That's why this book exists. It is designed to make that thoughtful hour easier, to give a little structure and focus to a study of the life and teachings of Christ. Whether you work through the pages as part of a group study or on your own, you will find a fresh look at the Beatitudes Jesus shared that day. The questions can be answered as part of a discussion or in your own heart as you read in thoughtful consideration.

Each of us learns differently. Many of us have loved the heart-touching account of the Sermon on the Mount found in Ellen White's *Thoughts From the Mount of Blessing.* Those poetic passages have lifted our minds to a higher level, opening before us the teachings of heaven and the struggles of life.

Others have struggled with the language level in *Thoughts From the Mount of Blessing.* For that reason, this book includes selections from *Blessings,* the modern language adaptation of *Thoughts From the Mount of Blessing.* The simpler vocabulary and shorter sentences and paragraphs have helped many grasp the lessons Jesus taught that day as they have not been able to before.

As each chapter of this book opens, you will see which Scripture passages are referenced. You can also see which chapters of *Thoughts From the Mount of Blessing* (and *Blessings*) tell the same story. From there, an introduction leads you into the study. You are encouraged to "in imagination go back to that scene" as you grapple with what the people heard that day by the lake, what they must have thought, and what Jesus meant for them to learn.

Then you will be invited to "Reflect on the story" as you read a selection from *Thoughts From the Mount of Blessing.* "Questions to consider" follows the selection, and invites you to review what you read, apply your imagination to the scenes, and apply what you read to your life today. A second selection to read will come from *Blessings,* with more questions to consider. Each selection will have the pages referenced from both *Thoughts From the Mount of Blessing* and *Blessings,* so that you can read the version you choose.

In your study or your group's study, you may find that you cover a chapter of the book each day. Or you may find that some chapters lead to more reading and more discussion. Approach the study at your own pace and dwell on each of the Beatitudes until the Holy Spirit has opened them up to you with life-changing power. There is much more than could be read in Scripture and in the writings of Ellen White. There are many other questions that could be asked. Study until the questions in your heart are answered.

It is my prayer that in your "thoughtful hours," you will find that the scene on that hillside by the lake comes alive in your imagination. May Jesus' words that day open your eyes to the kingdom He promised and make His words as real and as life-changing to you as they were to those who were there that day.

On the Hillside by the Lake 1

This study is based on Matthew 4:23–25 and
Thoughts From the Mount of Blessing, chapter 1
—see also *Blessings,* chapter 1.

A morning to remember

As the dawn broke that morning, the disciples began to stir. Looking about, it was clear that Jesus had not slept in His spot on the ground near them. Where was He?

It wasn't unusual for Jesus to be missing when the disciples woke up. He often spent the night in prayer rather than sleeping. In the quiet of the dark hours, He communed with His Father, preparing for the coming day and planning how to fulfill His mission to save humankind.

On this night, Jesus had been praying for His disciples. Knowing that His time on earth was short, He longed to see them prepared to carry on His work and take His gospel of love to the world. But with their limited education and long years of listening to the misguided Pharisees and leaders, they had much to learn.

Jesus approached them in the early morning light and gathered them into a circle. This time, as He spoke words of instruction and encouragement, He placed His hands on each of their heads and blessed them, asking His Father to enlighten their minds with understanding so that they could light the world with love. He dedicated each one to the work of sharing His gospel beginning on that day and lasting through every day for the rest of their lives.

From their secluded spot, Jesus led the group down to the lakeshore, where the waves lapped gently against the sand. Already a large crowd of people had gathered. They came from all the local towns in Galilee, from Jerusalem, where Jesus has recently visited, and from Decapolis, the heathen region on the other side of the lake. People had traveled from the far south and even from the great Phoenician cities of Tyre and Sidon on the shores of the Mediterranean. There was no room on the shore for such a crowd, so Jesus led them back up the hillside to where there was a mostly level spot where all could sit.

The people hadn't gathered that morning to hear a sermon. Many had come hoping to be healed of their illnesses or injuries. But mostly they had gathered because they hoped that Jesus was the long-awaited Messiah. They hoped to hear Him proclaim Himself their King and declare them free from the hated Romans.

Even the disciples felt that something exciting was going to happen. Jesus' actions that morning made them think that this might be the day He would announce His plans to become King. Everyone imagined the day when Israel would be the most powerful nation on earth and all would bow before them.

The Pharisees imagined ruling over the Romans and claiming their great riches. The peasants and fishermen wanted nothing more than to hear that their days of hard work would soon be over. They pictured living in mansions, wearing the luxurious robes of the Romans instead of their soiled cloaks as their no-longer-hungry children played happily.

There they sat, thousands of people, each with their own dream of what the future would bring. As Jesus opened His mouth to speak, they turned with eager expectation.

But Jesus had something else in mind.

Reflect on the story

"More than fourteen centuries before Jesus was born in Bethlehem, the children of Israel gathered in the fair vale of Shechem, and from the mountains on either side the voices of the priests were heard proclaiming the blessings and the curses—'a blessing, if ye obey the commandments of the Lord your God: . . . and a curse, if ye will not obey.' Deuteronomy 11:27, 28. And thus the mountain from which the words of benediction were spoken came to be known as the mount of blessing. But it was not upon Gerizim that the words were spoken which have come as a benediction to a sinning and sorrowing world. Israel fell short of the high ideal which had been set before her. Another than Joshua must guide His people to the true rest of faith. No longer is Gerizim known as the mount of the Beatitudes, but that unnamed mountain beside the Lake of Gennesaret, where Jesus spoke the words of blessing to His disciples and the multitude.

"Let us in imagination go back to that scene, and, as we sit with the disciples on the mountainside, enter into the thoughts and feelings that filled their hearts. Understanding what the words of Jesus meant to those who heard them, we may discern in them a new vividness and beauty, and may also gather for ourselves their deeper lessons.

"When the Saviour began His ministry, the popular conception of the Messiah and His work was such as wholly unfitted the people to receive Him. The spirit of true devotion had been lost in tradition and ceremonialism, and the prophecies were interpreted at the dictate of proud, world-loving hearts. The Jews looked for the coming One, not as a Saviour from sin, but as a great prince who should bring all nations under the supremacy of the Lion of the tribe of Judah. In vain had John the Baptist, with the heart-searching power of the ancient prophets, called them to repentance. In vain had he, beside the Jordan, pointed to Jesus as the Lamb of God, that taketh away the sin of the world. God was seeking to direct their minds to Isaiah's prophecy of the suffering Saviour, but they would not hear.

"Had the teachers and leaders in Israel yielded to His transforming grace, Jesus would have made them His ambassadors among men. In Judea first the coming of the kingdom had been proclaimed, and the call to repentance had been given. In the act of driving out the desecrators from the temple at Jerusalem, Jesus had announced Himself as the Messiah—the One who should cleanse the soul from the defilement of sin and make His people a holy temple unto the Lord. But the Jewish leaders would not humble themselves to receive the lowly Teacher from Nazareth. At His second visit to Jerusalem He was arraigned before the Sanhedrin, and fear of the people alone prevented these dignitaries from trying to take His life. Then it was that, leaving Judea, He entered upon His ministry in Galilee.

"His work there had continued some months before the Sermon on the Mount was given. The message He had proclaimed throughout the land, 'The kingdom of heaven is at hand' (Matthew 4:17), had arrested the attention of all classes, and had still further fanned the flame of their ambitious hopes.

The fame of the new Teacher had spread beyond the limits of Palestine, and, notwithstanding the attitude of the hierarchy, the feeling was widespread that this might be the hoped-for Deliverer. Great multitudes thronged the steps of Jesus, and the popular enthusiasm ran high" (*Thoughts From the Mount of Blessing*, 1–3; see also *Blessings,* 11–13).

Questions to consider

1. How can we learn to see a new vividness and beauty in the words of Jesus? Is it possible for us to misunderstand Jesus as badly as the people of His time did?

2. Could we be in danger of also losing the spirit of true devotion to tradition and ceremonials? What traditions and ceremonies have filled our worship today?

3. What message did Jesus exclaim in Galilee in the months leading up to the Sermon on the Mount? What did the people understand that to mean? What did it really mean?

Reflect on the story

"Now it was time for His closest disciples to join in His work, helping to care for the large crowds who followed Jesus. Some of the disciples had been with Jesus since the beginning of His ministry, and nearly all twelve had traveled and lived with Him like members of a family. But they had also been misled by the teachings of the rabbis so that, like the crowds, they expected Jesus to establish Himself soon as King of Israel. With this expectation, they couldn't understand what Jesus was doing. Why didn't He seek the support of the priests and rabbis? Why was He doing nothing to establish His authority as King?

"These disciples had much to learn before Jesus could leave them with the responsibility for His church on earth. But they had responded to Jesus' love, and He saw that He could train and teach them even though they were slow to see the truth of God's kingdom. They had been with Him long enough to begin to believe that He was on a divine mission from God. Many of the huge crowds that followed Jesus had seen much of His power. Now it was time to teach them all the principles of His kingdom.

"Alone on a hilltop near the Sea of Galilee, Jesus spent all night in prayer for His chosen disciples. At dawn, He called them together and shared important lessons with them. He prayed with them and laid His hands on their heads and blessed them, dedicating them to the gospel work. Then He led them to the edge of the lake, where even at that early morning hour, a massive crowd was already gathering.

"Besides the usual throngs of people from the towns in Galilee, a great many others had gathered as well—from Judea, Jerusalem, and half-pagan Decapolis; from far to the south and from Tyre and Sidon, the Phoenician cities on the shore of the Mediterranean. 'They all came to hear Jesus teach and to be healed of their sicknesses' (Luke 6:18 [NCV]).

"There wasn't enough room on the narrow lakeshore for everyone who wanted to hear Jesus, so He led them back to the hillside. At a level spot where there was room for everyone, Jesus sat down on the grass. His disciples and the crowd of people did the same.

"The disciples stayed close to their Master, feeling that something unusual was about to happen. Jesus' actions earlier that morning made them think that He was going to announce His plans to become King. The people felt the excitement as well, and each person waited eagerly for Jesus' words. As they sat on the green hillside, they were filled with thoughts of their nation's future glory and power. Among them were scribes and Pharisees who looked forward to the day when they would rule over the hated Romans and claim the riches of the world's great empire. The peasants and fishermen hoped to hear that their poor houses and days of hard work, worry, and hunger would soon be replaced with mansions and days of ease. They hoped to trade in the simple garment they wore as a coat by day and used as a blanket by night for the rich robes of the Romans.

"The heart of each person was filled with pride that Israel would soon be honored worldwide as God's chosen nation and that Jerusalem would be the capitol of the world."

But Jesus had a different mission and a different message (*Blessings,* 13–15; see also *Thoughts From the Mount of Blessing,* 3–5).

Questions to consider

1. Why was Jesus patient with the disciples even when they didn't understand His mission? What does that teach us about being patient with fellow church members who seem just as misled?

2. Why did Jesus lead the crowd away from the lake to the hillside? Why had so many people come that day?

3. The Pharisees longed for worldly power and honor. The peasants longed for escape from hunger and hard work. What do you long for most when you turn to Jesus?

Blessed Are the Poor in Spirit 2

This study is based on Matthew 5:1–12 and
Thoughts From the Mount of Blessing, chapter 2
—see also *Blessings,* chapter 2.

The Beatitudes

As Jesus began to speak that morning, His words were not what people were expecting or hoping for. He didn't talk about kings or kingdoms, about ruling the world or basking in riches. Instead His simple words spoke to their spiritual lives, to the issues they struggled with each day.

The word *blessed* in the Beatitudes can be translated as "happy." Jesus begins now to describe what kind of life is a "happy" life for a Christian. "Happy are those who are poor in spirit. The kingdom of heaven belongs to them."

The scribes and Pharisees must have rolled their eyes in annoyance at the idea. They considered themselves rich in spirit, thanking God that they weren't like the sin-filled unwashed masses around them. Of course they were members of God's kingdom! How could they not be? There could be no advantage in being "poor" in anything.

Among the peasants and fishermen, some must have looked around with a quizzical look on their faces. They were certainly "poor in spirit." They felt far from God, assuming that their sins made them unacceptable compared to others. Could they really be part of the kingdom of heaven? Was it possible that God actually valued them? Hope began to rise in their hearts.

They might have been expecting a kingdom on earth, but what Jesus offered that morning was the kingdom of heaven—a kingdom of love, of grace, of forgiveness. By recognizing their need of God, they qualified to be citizens of heaven. Being poor in spirit, they were blessed—they could be happy.

Perhaps their dreams of being part of a privileged kingdom on earth didn't evaporate immediately, but the idea—the promise—that they might be citizens of the kingdom of heaven began to grow in their hearts. In spite of the looks of those around them, regardless of the dazzling morning sun, they began to focus on what Jesus would say next.

The scribes and Pharisees settled under their rich robes with a weary sigh. Jesus was proving again to be just a rabble-rouser, a troublemaker determined to stir up the people with false promises and hope. Their vision of the kingdom of heaven didn't include most of these wretched people, and it certainly didn't include Jesus.

The disciples may have been most puzzled of all. They weren't hearing any announcement of a political takeover, but Jesus was speaking of a kingdom. They recognized the sincerity in Jesus' voice. Could He really mean that any of these people, everyone in this crowd, could be a part of His kingdom? The morning had begun with such promise—could it be that Jesus' kingdom of heaven was not the kingdom on earth they hoped for? Could they have been wrong about Him being the Messiah?

Reflect on the story

" 'He opened His mouth, and taught them, saying, Blessed are the poor in spirit: for theirs is the kingdom of heaven.' Matthew 5:2, 3.

"As something strange and new, these words fall upon the ears of the wondering multitude. Such teaching is contrary to all they have ever heard from priest or rabbi. They see in it nothing to flatter their pride or to feed their ambitious hopes. But there is about this new Teacher a power that holds them spellbound. The sweetness of divine love flows from His very presence as the fragrance from a flower. His words fall like 'rain upon the mown grass: as showers that water the earth.' Psalm 72:6. All feel instinctively that here is One who reads the secrets of the soul, yet who comes near to them with tender compassion. Their hearts open to Him, and, as they listen, the Holy Spirit unfolds to them something of the meaning of that lesson which humanity in all ages so needs to learn.

"In the days of Christ the religious leaders of the people felt that they were rich in spiritual treasure. The prayer of the Pharisee, 'God, I thank Thee, that I am not as the rest of men' (Luke 18:11, R.V.), expressed the feeling of his class and, to a great degree, of the whole nation. But in the throng that surrounded Jesus there were some who had a sense of their spiritual poverty. When in the miraculous draft of fishes the divine power of Christ was revealed, Peter fell at the Saviour's feet, exclaiming, 'Depart from me; for I am a sinful man, O Lord' (Luke 5:8); so in the multitude gathered upon the mount there were souls who, in the presence of His purity, felt that they were 'wretched, and miserable, and poor, and blind, and naked' (Revelation 3:17); and they longed for 'the grace of God that bringeth salvation' (Titus 2:11). In these souls, Christ's words of greeting awakened hope; they saw that their lives were under the benediction of God.

"Jesus had presented the cup of blessing to those who felt that they were 'rich, and increased with goods' (Revelation 3:17), and had need of nothing, and they had turned with scorn from the gracious gift. He who feels whole, who thinks that he is reasonably good, and is contented with his condition, does not seek to become a partaker of the grace and righteousness of Christ. Pride feels no need, and so it closes the heart against Christ and the infinite blessings He came to give. There is no room for Jesus in the heart of such a person. Those who are rich and honorable in their own eyes do not ask in faith, and receive the blessing of God. They feel that they are full, therefore they go away empty. Those who know that they cannot possibly save themselves, or of themselves do any righteous action, are the ones who appreciate the help that Christ can bestow. They are the poor in spirit, whom He declares to be blessed" (*Thoughts From the Mount of Blessing*, 6, 7; see also *Blessings*, 16, 17).

Questions to consider

1. What does "poor in spirit" mean to you? Shouldn't "rich in spirit" be better?

2. The religious leaders of the day thought that they were "rich in spirit." When have you felt "rich in spirit"? Is it possible for church leaders today to feel that way?

3. How can we avoid spiritual pride? What is the difference between feeling spiritual pride and putting effort into living right? Shouldn't we strive to live right and encourage others to do so?

Reflect on the story

"Jesus forgives, but through the Holy Spirit, He also leads us to feel sorrow for our sins and to ask for forgiveness. The Spirit leads us to see that have nothing good in ourselves and that even the good we have done is mingled with selfishness and sin. Like the poor tax collector, we stand off with our eyes looking down and say, ' "God, have mercy on me, a sinner" ' (Luke 18:13 [NCV]). Because we acknowledge our need, we are blessed and our sins are forgiven. God's promise is, 'Though your sins are like scarlet, they can be as white as snow. Though your sins are deep red, they can be white like wool' (Isaiah 1:18 [NCV]). And beyond just forgiving us, God also promises to give us a new heart.

"Jesus didn't promise the spiritually needy an earthly kingdom, but a spiritual kingdom of His love, His grace, and His righteousness. As subjects of His kingdom, we are being changed—we are becoming like Him and ready 'to have a share in all that he has prepared for his people in the kingdom of light' (Colossians 1:12 [NCV]).

"If you sense something missing in your own soul, if you feel that you have nothing good inside, you can find goodness and strength in Jesus. You're not worthy of God's love, but Jesus *is* worthy, and He will save everyone who comes to Him. Whatever is in your past, however discouraging things may be at this moment, you can come to Jesus. You can come to Him just as you are—weak-willed, guilty, and depressed—and He will meet you with open arms. He will place His robe of righteousness around you and present you to His Father, saying, 'I have taken this sinner's place. Don't look at his life, but at Mine' " (*Blessings*, 17, 18; see also *Thoughts From the Mount of Blessing*, 7–9).

Questions to consider

1. How do we find happiness when we know our situation as sinners?

2. What does it mean to be a citizen of the kingdom of heaven? How would the citizen be identifiable?

3. Have you been able to come to Jesus, and believe that He meets you with open arms? Can you let go of your past and accept His robe of righteousness?

Blessed Are Those Who Mourn   3

This study is based on Matthew 5:1–12 and
Thoughts From the Mount of Blessing, chapter 2
—see also *Blessings,* chapter 2.

Is there blessing in pain?

How many people sitting on the hillside were in pain? Certainly many had come to find Jesus for healing. If you were suffering with an incurable or painful disease or injury today, how far would you travel if you heard of someone who could heal you? How far would you travel if someone you loved was suffering?

Imagine your pain that morning if you had traveled far to see Jesus, but just before dawn, your loved one had died. Days, weeks, months on the road, only to fail at the last moment. Sitting on the hillside that morning, you would overlook the golden sunlight. You wouldn't hear the singing of birds or notice the beautiful aroma of wildflowers. No matter the mood of those around you, you would be mourning.

"Blessed are they that mourn, for they shall be comforted" is hard to hear when you've lost someone you love. What was Jesus trying to say that morning? What blessing comes to those who mourn?

In a world of sin and death, there is no doubt that sorrow will find us. God does not promise that faith in Him will prevent sorrow. He promises that faith will allow us to deal with sorrow. Faith allows us to find joy and hope again.

And the sorrow of loss can be a blessing if it turns us to God. "The trials of life are God's workmen, to remove the impurities and roughness from our character." If difficulty, sorrow, and loss turn us toward God, they are a blessing. If they have strengthened our faith, renewed our commitment to living right, and taught us the importance of treating others with love, then they have indeed left us better, happier people.

If we had sat there that morning and followed Jesus' steps from that place to the cross, we would know for certain that He understands our sorrow. He was human, like we are, and pain and sorrow afflicted Him each day. He wept at the death of His friend Lazarus, even knowing that Lazarus would soon rise and live again. We can be sure that He feels our pain and understands the human heart.

On the hillside that morning, Jesus' words were focused on the sorrow that comes with realizing that we have sinned—and what that sin cost the Savior. And that kind of mourning can only be comforted when we turn to Jesus for forgiveness and salvation. When our mourning over our lives turns us to Jesus, it becomes a blessing.

Reflect on the story

> " 'Blessed are they that mourn: for they shall be comforted.'
> Matthew 5:4.

"The mourning here brought to view is true heart sorrow for sin. Jesus says, 'I, if I be lifted up from the earth, will draw all men unto Me.' John 12:32. And as one is drawn to behold Jesus uplifted on the cross, he discerns the sinfulness of humanity. He sees that it is sin which scourged and crucified the Lord of glory. He sees that, while he has been loved with unspeakable tenderness, his life has been a continual scene of ingratitude and rebellion. He has forsaken his best Friend and abused heaven's most precious gift. He has crucified to himself the Son of God afresh and pierced anew that bleeding and stricken heart. He is separated from God by a gulf of sin that is broad and black and deep, and he mourns in brokenness of heart.

"Such mourning 'shall be comforted.' God reveals to us our guilt that we may flee to Christ, and through Him be set free from the bondage of sin, and rejoice in the liberty of the sons of God. In true contrition we may come to the foot of the cross, and there leave our burdens.

"The Saviour's words have a message of comfort to those also who are suffering affliction or bereavement. Our sorrows do not spring out of the ground. God 'doth not afflict willingly nor grieve the children of men.' Lamentations 3:33. When He permits trials and afflictions, it is 'for our profit, that we might be partakers of His holiness.' Hebrews 12:10. If received in faith, the trial that seems so bitter and hard to bear will prove a blessing. The cruel blow that blights the joys of earth will be the means of turning our eyes to heaven. How many there are who would never have known Jesus had not sorrow led them to seek comfort in Him!

"The trials of life are God's workmen, to remove the impurities and roughness from our character. Their hewing, squaring, and chiseling, their burnishing and polishing, is a painful process; it is hard to be pressed down to the grinding wheel. But the stone is brought forth prepared to fill its place in the heavenly temple. Upon no useless material does the Master bestow such careful, thorough work. Only His precious stones are polished after the similitude of a palace.

"The Lord will work for all who put their trust in Him. Precious victories will be gained by the faithful. Precious lessons will be learned. Precious experiences will be realized.

"Our heavenly Father is never unmindful of those whom sorrow has touched. When David went up the Mount Olivet, 'and wept as he went up, and had his head covered, and he went barefoot' (2 Samuel 15:30), the Lord was looking pityingly upon him. David was clothed in sackcloth, and his conscience was scourging him. The outward signs of humiliation testified of his contrition. In tearful, heartbroken utterances he presented his case to God, and the Lord did not forsake His servant. Never was David dearer to the heart of Infinite Love than when, conscience-smitten, he fled for his life from his enemies, who had been stirred to rebellion by his own son. The Lord says, 'As many as I love, I rebuke and chasten: be zealous therefore, and repent.' Revelation 3:19. Christ lifts up the contrite heart and refines the mourning soul until it becomes His abode.

"But when tribulation comes upon us, how many of us are like Jacob! We think it the hand of an enemy; and in the darkness we wrestle blindly until our strength is spent, and we find no comfort or deliverance. To Jacob the divine touch at break of day revealed the One with whom he had been contending—the Angel of the covenant; and, weeping and helpless, he fell upon the breast of Infinite Love, to receive the blessing for which his soul longed. We also need to learn that trials mean benefit, and not to despise the chastening of the Lord nor faint when we are rebuked of Him" (*Thoughts From the Mount of Blessing*, 9–11; see also *Blessings*, 18–20).

Questions to consider

1. Why would a believer mourn? How can we be comforted?

2. "The trials of life are God's workmen." What does that mean?

3. How is it that we are like Jacob when trials come to us? What do we need to learn as he did?

Reflect on the story

" 'The one whom God corrects is happy, so do not hate being corrected by the Almighty. God hurts, but he also bandages up; he injures, but his hands also heal' (Job 5:17, 18 [NCV]). Jesus offers His healing love to each person who is sick or injured. Those whose lives are plagued by grief, pain, and loss can choose to feel Jesus' presence in their suffering.

"God doesn't want us to remain beaten down by sorrowful, breaking hearts. We can look up and see the love on His face. Many whose eyes are blinded by tears fail to see that Jesus is standing right beside them. He wants so much for us to reach out with a simple faith that will let Him guide us. His heart is touched by our sorrow and our troubles. His everlasting love surrounds us, and we can meditate on that love all through the day. He will lift us above our troubles to a world of peace. Faith allows us to deal with our sorrow and to find joy and hope again.

"This blessing is also promised to those who join Jesus in weeping for the pain and sin in the world. Jesus suffered great anguish on His path to save the world. The sin and selfishness around Him bruised His spirit. He worked so hard and suffered so much—only to see too many turn away from His offer of salvation. Each person who follows Him will feel some of this same pain. As we discover His love, we will join in His mission to save the lost. As we share in Jesus' sorrow and His mission, we will also share in His joy and glory.

"Because Jesus suffered as a human, He knows how to console us when we are in pain. Because He was tempted to sin, He can save us when we are tempted. Because Jesus has saved us, we can minister to those around us who fall into sin and experience pain.

"God has a special place in His heart for those who mourn, for He knows that sadness can melt hearts and help to save souls. His love opens a channel into our wounded souls and offers hope and healing to everyone who sorrows. 'Praise be to the God and Father of our Lord Jesus Christ. God is the Father who is full of mercy and all comfort. He comforts us every time we have trouble, so when others have trouble, we can comfort them with the same comfort God gives us' (2 Corinthians 1:3, 4 [NCV])" (*Blessings,* 20, 21; see also *Thoughts From the Mount of Blessing,* 12, 13).

Questions to consider

1. What is it that we can miss when our eyes are blinded by tears? What allows us to deal with our sorrows?

2. What does it mean to join in Jesus' sorrow and His mission? How have you experienced this in your life?

3. Why does God have a special place in His heart for those who mourn? Can this bring us any comfort?

Blessed Are the Meek   4

This study is based on Matthew 5:1–12 and
Thoughts From the Mount of Blessing, chapter 2
—see also *Blessings,* chapter 2.

A pathway to God

With the green hillside at His back and the blue sky above, Jesus spoke to the gathered people. It wasn't the kind of sermon they were accustomed to hearing. In most synagogues of the day, a sermon consisted of someone reading a passage from the Torah—the books of the law in the Old Testament—and perhaps commenting on how the law should be kept. The tradition of Jewish rabbis was to explore a variety of possible interpretations, leaving the people with more of a philosophy of life than a message from God.

On the other hand, the scribes and Pharisees taught a very strict interpretation of the law. They taught rules about how many steps one could take on a Sabbath day, how one must pay tithe on a handful of seeds, and how offering must be given at the temple.

But on this bright morning, Jesus taught something very different. He shared the way to live as a true follower of God. He showed how to become a citizen of the kingdom of God.

The Beatitudes are, in many ways, a pathway for the growing Christian. They are steps to leaving behind a world of pride, of selfishness, of anger and hate. On this path, we start by recognizing what we need—a pure heart—and recognizing that we don't have it. Next we see that sin and rebellion against God bring sadness and pain—reasons to mourn. But the sadness can turn our hearts to God.

The next step has to do with how we live, how we treat those around us. "Blessed are the meek" or the gentle, for they will be the ones who possess the earth in the end.

So many people in the crowd that day wished for nothing more than to own the earth. They wanted to destroy the Roman Empire and force the other cities and civilizations of earth to bow down to them. They wanted power over all people, and the riches that would come with such power. And they saw only one way to achieve that goal—by force.

The scenario must have danced through the minds of peasants and Pharisees alike. Jesus would announce His kingship and take the throne in Jerusalem. Jews everywhere would flock to His cause, and His army would number in the thousands. With Jesus the Messiah at its head, the army would be unstoppable. The Roman legions would fall before them as Jesus healed any of His soldiers who were injured or killed. Miraculously providing food each day, Jesus would lead the march on Rome and overthrow Caesar himself. Soon all nations would come and bow before them, and Israel would take its rightful place as the ruler of the world.

But Jesus turned that scenario upside down. The meek would inherit the earth, not the strong, ambitious, or forceful. Gentleness was no more popular as a character trait in those days than it is today. Successful, powerful men and women are never described as gentle. But Jesus said that a true Christian should live that way.

Living with gentleness means giving up pride and ambition. It means living at peace with others no matter how we are treated. It means living like Jesus did.

Reflect on the story

" 'Blessed are those who are gentle. They will inherit the earth'
(Matthew 5:5, God's Word).

"This part of Jesus' sermon—the Beatitudes—shows us the path of a growing Christian. First, we recognize our spiritual need. Then we find that sin brings sadness, but this sadness can be a blessing because it shows us our need for Jesus. Next, we learn about being gentle or meek.

"Patience and meekness—the ability to respond gently even when we are wronged—were not character traits appreciated by the Jews of Jesus' day or by the other nations on earth. Under the inspiration of the Holy Spirit, Moses claimed to be the meekest man on earth, but that didn't strike the people of his day as a good thing. Instead, they viewed meekness with pity or a sneer. But Jesus listed gentleness as one of the important qualifications for His kingdom—and showed gentleness in His own life.

"Jesus was the Divine Ruler of heaven, but He gave it up and became a humble, created human—a servant. He walked among human beings not as a king demanding honor, but as a servant on a mission. He didn't act as if He were better or more important than any other person. The Savior of the world was superior to angels, but the humble way He lived and interacted with people made Him Someone they wanted to be around.

"Jesus gave up His own interests and His own plans. Nothing that He did on earth was for Himself. He lived only to do His Father's will. When His mission on earth was almost over, Jesus could say to His Father, 'Having finished the work you gave me to do, I brought you glory on earth' (John 17:4 [NCV]).

"Jesus says to us, 'Accept my teachings and learn from me, because I am gentle and humble in spirit' (Matthew 11:29 [NCV]). If we are going to follow Jesus, we must give up on self and selfishness. Like Jesus, we must live only to do our heavenly Father's will.

"When we witness Jesus' selflessness, His humility, we see that our self-sufficient independence comes from following Satan. It is human nature to clamor for attention, but as we follow Jesus, we learn to let go of our pride, our focus on ourselves, and our need to be in charge. No longer anxious to elbow our way to the top, we find that our highest place is at the feet of our Savior. We look to Jesus, waiting for His hand to lead us, listening for His voice to guide us. The apostle Paul had this experience. He tells us, 'I was put to death on the cross with Christ, and I do not live anymore—it is Christ who lives in me. I still live in my body, but I live by faith in the Son of God who loved me and gave himself to save me' (Galatians 2:20 [NCV]).

"Jesus' presence in our lives gives us an abiding sense of peace. Even though He was often surrounded by conflict, Jesus lived at peace. No storm of human or satanic anger could disturb the calm of His connection to God. To us He says, 'I leave you peace; my peace I give you. I do not give it to you as the world does. So don't let your hearts be troubled or afraid' (John 14:27 [NCV])" (*Blessings,* 21–23; see also *Thoughts From the Mount of Blessing,* 13–15).

Questions to consider

1. What does it mean to be gentle or meek? Is gentleness seen as a positive thing today? Who is someone you would describe as gentle or meek?

2. How did Jesus live in a gentle way? Can we live that way also?

3. How can living gently or meekly bring us peace? What can you do to have more peace in your life?

Reflect on the story

"It is the love of self that destroys our peace. While self is all alive, we stand ready continually to guard it from mortification and insult; but when we are dead, and our life is hid with Christ in God, we shall not take neglects or slights to heart. We shall be deaf to reproach and blind to scorn and insult. 'Love suffereth long, and is kind; love envieth not; love vaunteth not itself, is not puffed up, doth not behave itself unseemly, seeketh not its own, is not provoked, taketh not account of evil; rejoiceth not in unrighteousness, but rejoiceth with the truth; beareth all things, believeth all things, hopeth all things, endureth all things. Love never faileth.' 1 Corinthians 13:4-8, R.V.

"Happiness drawn from earthly sources is as changeable as varying circumstances can make it; but the peace of Christ is a constant and abiding peace. It does not depend upon any circumstances in life, on the amount of worldly goods or the number of earthly friends. Christ is the fountain of living water, and happiness drawn from Him can never fail.

"The meekness of Christ, manifested in the home, will make the inmates happy; it provokes no quarrel, gives back no angry answer, but soothes the irritated temper and diffuses a gentleness that is felt by all within its charmed circle. Wherever cherished, it makes the families of earth a part of the one great family above.

"Far better would it be for us to suffer under false accusation than to inflict upon ourselves the torture of retaliation upon our enemies. The spirit of hatred and revenge originated with Satan, and can bring only evil to him who cherishes it. Lowliness of heart, that meekness which is the fruit of abiding in Christ, is the true secret of blessing. 'He will beautify the meek with salvation.' Psalm 149:4.

"The meek 'shall inherit the earth.' It was through the desire for self-exaltation that sin entered into the world, and our first parents lost the dominion over this fair earth, their kingdom. It is through self-abnegation that Christ redeems what was lost. And He says we are to overcome as He did. Revelation 3:21. Through humility and self-surrender we may become heirs with Him when 'the meek shall inherit the earth.' Psalm 37:11.

"The earth promised to the meek will not be like this, darkened with the shadow of death and the curse. 'We, according to His promise, look for new heavens and a new earth, wherein dwelleth righteousness.' 'There shall be no more curse: but the throne of God and of the Lamb shall be in it; and His servants shall serve Him.' 2 Peter 3:13; Revelation 22:3.

"There is no disappointment, no sorrow, no sin, no one who shall say, I am sick; there are no burial trains, no mourning, no death, no partings, no broken hearts; but Jesus is there, peace is there. There 'they shall not hunger nor thirst; neither shall the heat nor sun smite them: for He that hath mercy on them shall lead them, even by the springs of water shall He guide them.' Isaiah 49:10" (*Thoughts From the Mount of Blessing*, 16–18; see also *Blessings*, 23, 24).

Questions to consider

1. How does a love of self destroy our peace?

2. What does retaliating against those who have wronged us bring to us? Is there a time when it is only fair to retaliate?

3. The meek "inherit the earth" when Jesus returns. Is there a reward for the meek today?

Blessed Are Those Who Hunger and Thirst 5

This study is based on Matthew 5:1–12 and
Thoughts From the Mount of Blessing, chapter 2
—see also *Blessings,* chapter 2.

A matter of life and death

Among the crowd on the hillside that morning were people of all types, but many of them were peasants and fishermen from around Galilee. Peasants most often worked in the fields, planting or harvesting crops for wealthy landowners. It was hard, backbreaking labor, and the pay was barely enough to keep a family fed. Too often, there was no work to be done and the peasant's family went hungry.

Most of the fishermen on the Sea of Galilee were laborers also, working on boats owned by others with their pay completely dependent on the success of the fishing on any given day. When the fishing went poorly, the fisherman and his family went hungry.

For many on the hillside that morning, hunger and thirst were not just words—they and their children were often truly hungry and thirsty. Imagine their shock when Jesus said, "Happy are those who hunger and thirst . . ." For a moment, they may have thought Jesus was crazy. But as they listened, they realized what He was saying. Someone who truly hungered for righteousness—as they had hungered for food—was someone to whom righteousness was a life-and-death matter.

We need food to live. The energy we burn as we go through the day must be replenished or we die. Is it possible that we need spiritual food in the same way? Can it be that our spiritual energy must be replenished daily if we are to stay spiritually alive and connected to God?

A sense of spiritual need, a hunger for righteousness, is a blessing in our lives. When we recognize that something important is missing, we are willing to search for whatever it takes to fill the need in our hearts. When we hunger after the things of God, we are sure to be satisfied. We can be sure that the Holy Spirit is working to show us what is missing and what we can have if we will follow the path of Jesus.

When our hunger for righteousness is filled, we have something to share with others. Throughout His life, Jesus gave to others. He shared the love that His Father gave to Him. In the same way, we can share what we have been given by God with those we meet. We can share His love, His peace, His promises with all who cross our paths.

Hungering and thirsting after the things of God will bring us a measure of peace and love that can be found no other way. When we pursue God, we are promised that we will find Him.

Reflect on the story

> " 'Blessed are they which do hunger and thirst after righteousness: for
> they shall be filled.' Matthew 5:6.

"Righteousness is holiness, likeness to God, and 'God is love.' 1 John 4:16. It is conformity to the law of God, for 'all Thy commandments are righteousness' (Psalm 119:172), and 'love is the fulfilling of the law' (Romans 13:10). Righteousness is love, and love is the light and the life of God. The righteousness of God is embodied in Christ. We receive righteousness by receiving Him.

"Not by painful struggles or wearisome toil, not by gift or sacrifice, is righteousness obtained; but it is freely given to every soul who hungers and thirsts to receive it. 'Ho, every one that thirsteth, come ye to the waters, and he that hath no money; come ye, buy, and eat, . . . without money and without price.' 'Their righteousness is of Me, saith the Lord,' and, 'This is His name whereby He shall be called, THE LORD OUR RIGHTEOUSNESS.' Isaiah 55:1; 54:17; Jeremiah 23:6.

"No human agent can supply that which will satisfy the hunger and thirst of the soul. But Jesus says, 'Behold, I stand at the door, and knock: if any man hear My voice, and open the door, I will come in to him, and will sup with him, and he with Me.' 'I am the bread of life: he that cometh to Me shall never hunger; and he that believeth on Me shall never thirst.' Revelation 3:20; John 6:35.

"As we need food to sustain our physical strength, so do we need Christ, the Bread from heaven, to sustain spiritual life and impart strength to work the works of God. As the body is continually receiving the nourishment that sustains life and vigor, so the soul must be constantly communing with Christ, submitting to Him and depending wholly upon Him.

"As the weary traveler seeks the spring in the desert and, finding it, quenches his burning thirst, so will the Christian thirst for and obtain the pure water of life, of which Christ is the fountain.

"As we discern the perfection of our Saviour's character we shall desire to become wholly transformed and renewed in the image of His purity. The more we know of God, the higher will be our ideal of character and the more earnest our longing to reflect His likeness. A divine element combines with the human when the soul reaches out after God and the longing heart can say, 'My soul, wait thou only upon God; for my expectation is from Him.' Psalm 62:5.

"If you have a sense of need in your soul, if you hunger and thirst after righteousness, this is an evidence that Christ has wrought upon your heart, in order that He may be sought unto to do for you, through the endowment of the Holy Spirit, those things which it is impossible for you to do for yourself. We need not seek to quench our thirst at shallow streams; for the great fountain is just above us, of whose abundant waters we may freely drink, if we will rise a little higher in the pathway of faith" (*Thoughts From the Mount of Blessing*, 18, 19; see also *Blessings*, 24, 25).

Questions to consider

1. How is righteousness the same as love? Is it possible to be righteous but not be loving? Can we show love to others, but be unrighteous?

2. How does our need for physical food compare to our spiritual needs? Can we get by if we only eat food once a week? What if we are only spiritually fed once a week?

3. Where does a hunger and thirst for righteousness come from? Have you felt this hunger in your life?

Reflect on the story

"How can we know what Jesus wants from us? We can find those answers in the Bible, the Word of God. His words in the Bible are like springs of water, and drinking from them will bring us face to face with Jesus. As we begin to absorb His Word, certain verses and stories will light up with new meaning, and we will understand truth in new ways and see clearly how these truths relate to our salvation. We will know that Jesus is satisfying our hunger to know Him better.

"As the Holy Spirit helps us understand the Bible, we will be able to remember its truths and we will want to share them with others. Fresh, reassuring thoughts about the love of Jesus and His work in us will bubble up like water from a spring whenever we speak to others, whether or not they are fellow believers.

"The Bible says, 'Give and it will be given to you' (Luke 6:38, NIV), because God's blessings are like a fountain of water. When we drink from this fountain of love, we find ourselves wanting more. And as we share our growing understanding of Jesus' love, we understand it more and feel it more deeply. The more we know of God, the more we will be able to know and the more we can share His love with others. 'With God's power working in us, God can do much, much more than anything we can ask or imagine' (Ephesians 3:20 [NCV]).

"When Jesus left behind His life in heaven in order to come to our world and save us, He was given the unlimited help of the Holy Spirit. Each of Jesus' followers can have the same help if they will invite the Spirit to live in their hearts. God's command that we be filled with the Spirit is also a promise that we *will* be Spirit-filled if we surrender ourselves to Him.

"Like showers of rain that refresh the earth, God pours out His love to everyone on earth through the Holy Spirit" (*Blessings,* 25, 26; see also *Thoughts From the Mount of Blessing,* 20, 21).

Questions to consider

1. Where do we turn in order to understand what Jesus wants from us? Can you remember a time when your hunger for understanding life and God's plan was met in Scripture? What verse or passage spoke to you?

2. How is knowledge of God like a fountain? Have you felt God's love working in you? What have you done that you could not have done without that love?

Blessed Are the Merciful, the Pure in Heart, the Peacemakers   6

This study is based on Matthew 5:1–12 and
Thoughts From the Mount of Blessing, chapter 2
—see also *Blessings,* chapter 2.

A golden chain

As the people crowded onto the hillside that day, it was easy to see who the religious leaders were—they were the ones who paid no attention to those around them, who stepped on or over anyone who got in their way as they pushed to the front and sat nearest Jesus. You would have thought that being close to God meant having privileges that other "lesser" humans didn't have.

But back in the crowd, a fisherman helped an elderly woman make her way forward. A shopkeeper stopped to help a child who had fallen onto the ground. A poor farmer gave his spot to someone who had come seeking healing.

As we see too often today, it was not the religious leaders or those considered "righteous" that day who showed kindness or mercy to those around them. Peasants, shepherds, and merchants who were considered impure and cursed of God reached out to help those in need. It was to them that Jesus must have looked as He said, "Blessed are the merciful."

Like being gentle, being kind or merciful isn't usually considered the way to find success in this world. Our desire to "look out for number one" means that we must overlook the needs of others and focus on ourselves first. The worthiness of others, we think, is based on how much they can help us achieve our goals.

And like the Pharisees, it is easy for us to consider the less fortunate, the poor, the addicts, the criminals, and the abusers to be less worthy than ourselves. We believe that we have achieved value through our own efforts, our own hard work. We lose track of the fact that human value is determined by God and that our efforts mean nothing without Him.

When we glimpse our true relationship with God and the value He places on each of His children, we'll be able to stop looking down our noses at others "less fortunate" and asking, "Why bother helping?" Instead, we will only ask, "How can I help them?" The merciful or kind are blessed because when they show kindness, they give others a glimpse of God's character and God's love shines through them.

Being committed to helping others means being linked to God with a "golden chain of unbreakable promises." And those promises are that we will be shown kindness and mercy by God.

No doubt the Pharisees seated on the grass that morning felt pure. They had fulfilled the ceremonial rules and rites of purification. By their own standards, they were without sin. They could look around at the teeming crowd and smugly be sure that they were better than those pathetic people.

But Jesus did not suggest that purity was a function of ritual or rite. He did not suggest that a person could be pure by separating his or herself from the sinners around them. Jesus spoke to purity of the heart, a standard by which humans cannot measure. If we would see God, then we must be pure in heart by God's standards. And only one thing can make a human heart pure—the constant presence of the Holy Spirit.

As Jesus lived each day directed by the Holy Spirit, we can live with the Spirit guiding our plans, our thoughts, and our deeds. Being pure in heart doesn't mean we will never be tempted to sin. It means that we have surrendered our will to God, and that we allow the Holy Spirit to guide our footsteps.

To be pure of heart means to live each day in the presence of God—to live each day with the love of God shining through us.

Reflect on the story

> " 'Blessed are those who show mercy. They will be treated mercifully'
> (Matthew 5:7, God's Word).

"The human heart is naturally cold and selfish. Whenever someone shows kindness or mercy, it is because of the Holy Spirit's influence whether or not that person realizes it. God Himself is the Source of all mercy. He doesn't treat us as we deserve to be treated; He doesn't ask if we deserve to be loved. He just loves us, and that love gives us value and self-worth.

"God isn't spiteful or mean. He isn't trying to punish us—He's trying to save us. Even when He permits difficult or painful events to happen to us, He works through these things to lead us to Him and to salvation. He wants so much to relieve our suffering, to give us comfort and peace. God never excuses the guilty, but He does want to take away their guilt.

"When we show mercy, we share a bit of God's nature, and His love shines through us to others. When our hearts are connected to His heart of infinite love, we will also want to help people, not condemn them. Care and concern for others will continually flow out of our hearts if Jesus lives therein. Like Jesus, when we find others trapped and damaged by their own lifestyle choices, we won't ask, 'Are they worth helping?' Instead, we'll ask, 'How can I help them?' Even in the faces of the most depraved, most disgusting individuals, we will see only children of God in need of His love and saving grace.

"Showing mercy means helping the poor, the sick and injured, and those who are trapped, addicted, or overburdened. The Bible describes it like this: 'I saved the poor who called out and the orphan who had no one to help. The dying person blessed me, and I made the widow's heart sing. I put on right living as if it were clothing; I wore fairness like a robe and a turban. I was eyes for the blind and feet for the lame. I was like a father to needy people, and I took the side of strangers who were in trouble' (Job 29:12–16 [NCV]).

"Many people struggle their way through life in misery, certain that they are worthless and hopeless. To someone who is struggling and lonely, a kind word, a sympathetic look, a sincere 'thank you,' would be as welcome as a cup of cold water to someone dying of thirst. And every act of unselfish kindness expresses Jesus' love for lost humanity.

"There is a reward for those who show compassion for others. It comes in the peace and satisfaction of a life spent helping others. As the Bible teaches, we reap what we sow. 'Happy is the person who thinks about the poor. When trouble comes, the LORD will save him. The LORD will protect him and spare his life and will bless him in the land. He will not let his enemies take him. The LORD will give him strength when he is sick, and he will make him well again' (Psalm 41:1–3 [NCV]).

"If we dedicate our lives to helping others, we are linking ourselves to the God who holds the control of the universe in His hands. Our lives are tied to God with a golden chain of unbreakable promises—promises that will not be forgotten in our hour of need. The Bible says, 'My God will use his wonderful riches in Christ Jesus to give you everything you need' (Philippians 4:19 [NCV]). And when our lives finally come to an end, we will find a Savior of mercy eager to bring us one day to live with Him forever" (*Blessings*, 27–29; see also *Thoughts From the Mount of Blessing*, 21–24).

Questions to consider

1. "He doesn't treat us as we deserve to be treated; He doesn't ask if we deserve to be loved. He just loves us, and that love gives us value and self-worth." How has that love changed your life? How does that love help you to change the lives of others?

2. What does it mean to show mercy? Does your church have programs that show mercy this way? Should it?

3. Is your life tied to God with a golden chain of unbreakable promises? How does that make you feel?

Reflect on the story

" 'Blessed are the pure in heart: for they shall see God.' Matthew 5:8.

"The Jews were so exacting in regard to ceremonial purity that their regulations were extremely burdensome. Their minds were occupied with rules and restrictions and the fear of outward defilement, and they did not perceive the stain that selfishness and malice impart to the soul.

"Jesus does not mention this ceremonial purity as one of the conditions of entering into His kingdom, but points out the need of purity of heart. The wisdom that is from above 'is first pure.' James 3:17. Into the city of God there will enter nothing that defiles. All who are to be dwellers there will here have become pure in heart. In one who is learning of Jesus, there will be manifest a growing distaste for careless manners, unseemly language, and coarse thought. When Christ abides in the heart, there will be purity and refinement of thought and manner.

"But the words of Jesus, 'Blessed are the pure in heart,' have a deeper meaning—not merely pure in the sense in which the world understands purity, free from that which is sensual, pure from lust, but true in the hidden purposes and motives of the soul, free from pride and self-seeking, humble, unselfish, childlike.

"Only like can appreciate like. Unless you accept in your own life the principle of self-sacrificing love, which is the principle of His character, you cannot know God. The heart that is deceived by Satan, looks upon God as a tyrannical, relentless being; the selfish characteristics of humanity, even of Satan himself, are attributed to the loving Creator. 'Thou thoughtest,' He says, 'that I was altogether such an one as thyself.' Psalm 50:21. His providences are interpreted as the expression of an arbitrary, vindictive nature. So with the Bible, the treasure house of the riches of His grace. The glory of its truths, that are as high as heaven and compass eternity, is undiscerned. To the great mass of mankind, Christ Himself is 'as a root out of a dry ground,' and they see in Him 'no beauty that' they 'should desire Him.' Isaiah 53:2. When Jesus was among men, the revelation of God in humanity, the scribes and Pharisees declared to Him, 'Thou art a Samaritan, and hast a devil.' John 8:48. Even His disciples were so blinded by the selfishness of their hearts that they were slow to understand Him who had come to manifest to them the Father's love. This was why Jesus walked in solitude in the midst of men. He was understood fully in heaven alone.

"When Christ shall come in His glory, the wicked cannot endure to behold Him. The light of His presence, which is life to those who love Him, is death to the ungodly. The expectation of His coming is to them a 'fearful looking for of judgment and fiery indignation.' Hebrews 10:27. When He shall appear, they will pray to be hidden from the face of Him who died to redeem them.

"But to hearts that have become purified through the indwelling of the Holy Spirit, all is changed. These can know God. Moses was hid in the cleft of the rock when the glory of the Lord was revealed to him; and it is when we are hid in Christ that we behold the love of God.

" 'He that loveth pureness of heart, for the grace of his lips the King shall be his friend.' Proverbs 22:11. By faith we behold Him here and now. In our daily experience we discern His goodness and compassion in the manifestation of His providence. We recognize Him in the character of His Son. The Holy Spirit takes the truth concerning God and Him whom He hath sent, and opens it to the understanding and to the heart. The pure in heart see God in a new and endearing relation, as their Redeemer; and while they discern the purity and loveliness of His character, they long to reflect His image. They see Him as a Father longing to embrace a repenting son, and their hearts are filled with joy unspeakable and full of glory.

"The pure in heart discern the Creator in the works of His mighty hand, in the things of beauty that comprise the universe. In His written word they read in clearer lines the revelation of His mercy, His goodness, and His grace. The truths that are hidden from the wise and prudent are revealed to babes. The beauty and preciousness of truth, which are undiscerned by the worldly-wise, are constantly unfolding to those who have a trusting, childlike desire to know and to do the will of God. We discern the truth by becoming, ourselves, partakers of the divine nature.

"The pure in heart live as in the visible presence of God during the time He apportions them in this world. And they will also see Him face to face in the future, immortal state, as did Adam when he walked and talked with God in Eden. 'Now we see through a glass, darkly; but then face to face.' 1 Corinthians 13:12" (*Thoughts From the Mount of Blessing*, 24–27; see also *Blessings*, 29–31).

Questions to consider

1. Do we have measures of ceremonial purity similar to the Jews? Are there rules and regulations that are more important to us than caring for others?

2. What did "pure in heart" mean in Jesus' words? What does it mean to you today?

3. What must you do if you want to know God? What keeps you from doing this?

Reflect on the story

> " 'Blessed are those who make peace. They will be called God's children'
> (Matthew 5:9, God's Word).

"One of Jesus' titles is 'the Prince of Peace.' His mission is to bring peace back to earth and heaven. Sin destroyed that peace, but anyone who rejects sin and opens their heart to Jesus will share in the peace He brings.

"Jesus is the only Source of true peace. His presence in our hearts eases our pain and quiets our anger. A person who is at peace with God and with those around him cannot be made miserable. There will be no room in such a person's heart for envy or hatred or evil thoughts. The peace of God within the heart will spread its calming influence like refreshing dew to everyone around him.

"True followers of Jesus will share His message of peace with the world. Anyone who leads another person to God by showing Jesus' love in the way they live—in the things they do and say—is a peacemaker.

"The spirit of peace that fills Jesus' followers is clear evidence of His presence in their lives. The joy with which they live, the kindness they show toward others, and the integrity of their actions demonstrate to the world that they are Christians, true children of God. It is clear that they follow Jesus. As the Bible says, 'Everyone who loves has become God's child and knows God' (1 John 4:7 [NCV])" (*Blessings*, 32; see also *Thoughts From the Mount of Blessing*, 27, 28).

Questions to consider

1. "A person who is at peace with God and with those around him cannot be made miserable." Does that mean we should never be depressed? What about when depression is driven by a chemical imbalance?

2. Who appears to be a peacemaker in your church? What would your church be like if all the members were peacemakers?

_____

_____

Blessed Are the Persecuted 7

This study is based on Matthew 5:1–12 and
Thoughts From the Mount of Blessing, chapter 2
—see also *Blessings,* chapter 2.

The power of a life

No doubt many in the crowd that day felt that they had been persecuted. Roman soldiers infested their towns and villages, demanding the best food and lodging, treating Israelites like dogs. Many times, peasants were forced to work for a Roman soldier instead of working to provide food for their families. King Herod could impose his will on the Pharisees and Jewish rulers, compelling them to do as he wished. Others felt persecuted by those to whom they owed money. A person's home, their possessions, and even their family could be taken away in repayment of a debt.

How could someone who was persecuted feel blessed? Only if they were persecuted for righteousness' sake, Jesus said.

Jesus was certainly persecuted for righteousness' sake. He was accused, betrayed, abused, beaten, tortured, and killed, all because He followed the plan His Father had laid out for Him. And He doesn't promise that His followers won't experience the same. Anyone who shows the same love and kindness that Jesus showed, anyone who shares the same message of God's accepting love, will encounter opposition—resistance—and persecution.

Encountering these things may not be pleasant, but Jesus promises that they will be a blessing to us. They will strengthen our ties to Him and our desire to be in His kingdom.

Perhaps today we can identify better than we think with a peasant in the Galilean village. In those small communities, any rumor or lie told about you would be spread through the village in a flash. Soon everyone would be talking about you, criticizing you, even avoiding you, whether or not the rumor was true. Today, with the Internet and social media, a rumor about you can travel around the world before you even have the chance to deny it. And no matter what you say, some will always believe it to be true.

This is when our connection to Jesus is so important. No matter what lies are told about us, no matter what messages are sent, He knows what is true. If we have been faithful and honest and kind, then we can avoid panic or stress. The truth will come out someday. Through dependence on Jesus, we can be the same person whether people are shouting our praises or condemning us based on lies. By depending on Jesus, we can be like Him when the times are tough.

How we as Christians react when we are persecuted is one of the most powerful witnesses for the gospel. Showing faith and love when confronted by hate makes it clear to all who witness it that the love of God changes a person. It makes it clear that God's kingdom is something worth suffering for, worth dying for.

Even when confronted by grief and death in everyday life, the witness of a committed Christian is powerful. "If you can deal with the death of your loved one like that," many have heard, "then I want to know more about your beliefs, about your Jesus." Whether it's death, divorce, bankruptcy, loss of a job, or whatever tragedy that may befall us, our witness to those who know us is loud and clear. We can say, "My faith in God and His plan for my life help me deal with this tragedy. I don't know what tomorrow brings, but I know I can trust Him."

No more powerful words of witness can ever be spoken.

Reflect on the story

" 'Blessed are they which are persecuted for righteousness' sake: for theirs is the kingdom of heaven.' Matthew 5:10.

"Jesus does not present to His followers the hope of attaining earthly glory and riches, and of having a life free from trial, but He presents to them the privilege of walking with their Master in the paths of self-denial and reproach, because the world knows them not.

"He who came to redeem the lost world was opposed by the united forces of the adversaries of God and man. In an unpitying confederacy, evil men and evil angels arrayed themselves against the Prince of Peace. Though His every word and act breathed of divine compassion, His unlikeness to the world provoked the bitterest hostility. Because He would give no license for the exercise of the evil passions of our nature, He aroused the fiercest opposition and enmity. So it is with all who will live godly in Christ Jesus. Between righteousness and sin, love and hatred, truth and falsehood, there is an irrepressible conflict. When one presents the love of Christ and the beauty of holiness, he is drawing away the subjects of Satan's kingdom, and the prince of evil is aroused to resist it. Persecution and reproach await all who are imbued with the Spirit of Christ. The character of the persecution changes with the times, but the principle—the spirit that underlies it—is the same that has slain the chosen of the Lord ever since the days of Abel.

"As men seek to come into harmony with God, they will find that the offense of the cross has not ceased. Principalities and powers and wicked spirits in high places are arrayed against all who yield obedience to the law of heaven. Therefore, so far from causing grief, persecution should bring joy to the disciples of Christ, for it is an evidence that they are following in the steps of their Master.

"While the Lord has not promised His people exemption from trials, He has promised that which is far better. He has said, 'As thy days, so shall thy strength be.' 'My grace is sufficient for thee: for My strength is made perfect in weakness.' Deuteronomy 33:25; 2 Corinthians 12:9. If you are called to go through the fiery furnace for His sake, Jesus will be by your side even as He was with the faithful three in Babylon. Those who love their Redeemer will rejoice at every opportunity of sharing with Him humiliation and reproach. The love they bear their Lord makes suffering for His sake sweet.

"In all ages Satan has persecuted the people of God. He has tortured them and put them to death, but in dying they became conquerors. They revealed in their steadfast faith a mightier One than Satan. Satan could torture and kill the body, but he could not touch the life that was hid with Christ in God. He could incarcerate in prison walls, but he could not bind the spirit. They could look beyond the gloom to the glory, saying, 'I reckon that the sufferings of this present time are not worthy to be compared with the glory which shall be revealed in us.' 'Our light affliction, which is but for a moment, worketh for us a far more exceeding and eternal weight of glory.' Romans 8:18; 2 Corinthians 4:17.

"Through trials and persecution, the glory—character—of God is revealed in His chosen ones. The church of God, hated and persecuted by the world, are educated and disciplined in the school of Christ. They walk in narrow paths on earth; they are purified in the furnace of affliction. They follow Christ through sore conflicts; they endure self-denial and experience bitter disappointments; but their painful experience teaches them the guilt and woe of sin, and they look upon it with abhorrence. Being partakers of Christ's sufferings, they are destined to be partakers of His glory. In holy vision the prophet saw the triumph of the people of God. He says, 'I saw as it were a sea of glass mingled with fire: and them that had gotten the victory, . . . stand on the sea of glass, having the harps of God. And they sing the song of Moses the servant of God, and the song of the Lamb, saying, Great and marvelous are Thy works, Lord God Almighty; just and true are Thy ways, Thou King of saints.' 'These are they which came out of great tribulation, and have washed their robes, and made them white in the blood of the Lamb. Therefore are they before the throne of God, and serve Him day and night in His temple: and He that sitteth on the throne shall dwell among them.' Revelation 15:2, 3; 7:14, 15" (*Thoughts From the Mount of Blessing*, 29–31; see also *Blessings*, 33–35).

Questions to consider

1. Have you felt the oppression that comes with following Jesus? Does it bring you joy? Should it?

2. Rather than escaping trials and problems, what does God promise you and me?

3. Has the character of God been shown in your trials and tribulations? Why or why not?

Reflect on the story

" 'Blessed are you when people insult you, persecute you, lie, and say all kinds of evil things about you because of me' (Matthew 5:11, God's Word).

"Since the beginning, Satan has worked by deception. He has always tried to misrepresent God, and through his influence, he also misrepresents God's people today. No one was ever slandered more cruelly than was Jesus. He was insulted and mocked because He insisted on living solely by the principles of God's holy law. People hated Him for no reason. But still, He stood calmly before His enemies and declared that Christians can always expect criticism and hate. He showed His followers how to meet the hatred of the world and be encouraged to stand against it.

"Lies can damage our reputation, but they cannot stain our character. As long as we do not choose to sin, no one—satanic or human—can stain our souls. A person whose heart is committed to God is no different when facing the most difficult and discouraging situation than he is when all is well and God seems to be smiling upon him. Our words may be twisted, our motives maligned, even our actions may be misinterpreted, but this makes no real difference because we have bigger issues at risk. 'We set our eyes not on what we see but on what we cannot see. What we see will last only a short time, but what we cannot see will last forever' (2 Corinthians 4:18 [NCV]).

"When things are misunderstood or misrepresented, Jesus knows the truth. No matter what is said about us, we can wait patiently and trust Him because the truth will someday come to light. And those who have stood honorably with God will be honored by Him before the redeemed and angels.

"Jesus said, 'People will insult you and hurt you. They will lie and say all kinds of evil things about you because you follow me. But when they do, you will be happy. Rejoice and be glad, because you have a great reward waiting for you in heaven. People did the same evil things to the prophets who lived before you' (Matthew 5:11, 12 [NCV]). Adam's own faithful son, Abel, was killed because he was righteous. Enoch walked with God, but the world did not approve of him. Noah was mocked as a fanatic and a doomsayer. 'Some were laughed at and beaten. Others were put in chains and thrown into prison' (Hebrews 11:36 [NCV]).

"God's messengers have always been insulted and persecuted, but as a result, knowledge about God has spread even wider. Every follower of Christ should step forward and carry out the same work, knowing that everything done against God's people will help spread truth, not hold it back. God wants truth to be discussed and examined even if it involves persecution and criticism to make that happen. Every controversy, every criticism, every attempt to deny people spiritual freedom are part of God's plan to awaken sleeping minds.

"The history of God's messengers shows how true this is. When the Jewish Sanhedrin stirred up the crowd to stone Stephen to death, the message of the gospel was not hindered. Reports of how the light of heaven shone on Stephen's face as he died and the memory of the compassion in his final prayer, went like arrows into the hearts of those who witnessed his death and also into the hearts of those who heard the story.

"One of those arrows struck the heart of the Pharisee Saul, and he was transformed into a witness for Christ to Jews and Gentiles, even to kings. Long years later, Paul wrote from his prison cell in Rome: 'It is true that some preach about Christ because they are jealous and ambitious. . . . Others preach about Christ for selfish and wrong reasons, wanting to make trouble for me in prison. But it doesn't matter. The important thing is that in every way, whether for right or wrong reasons, they are preaching about Christ' (Philippians 1:15–18 [NCV]).

"Through Paul's imprisonment, the gospel was spread further, and people even within Caesar's palace become believers. The more Satan tries to destroy the seed of God's Word, the more firmly it is planted in human hearts. As Jesus' followers are cursed and imprisoned, His name is lifted up, and others become believers.

"Those who witness for Christ through persecution and criticism will be rewarded in heaven. But there is also reward in this life for all who follow God. To know God, to understand His purposes and His plans, to grasp more of His love, and glimpse more of His power is a treasure beyond human understanding. 'I pray that you and all God's holy people will have the power to understand the greatness of Christ's love—how wide and how long and how high and how deep that love is. Christ's love is greater than anyone can ever know, but I pray that you will be able to know that love. Then you can be filled with the fullness of God' (Ephesians 3:18, 19 [NCV]).

"This was the joy that filled Paul and Silas's hearts when they prayed and sang praises to God at midnight in a jail in Philippi. The light of Jesus' presence drove out the gloom and lifted them up. From his prison in Rome, Paul delighted to hear reports of the spreading gospel: 'So I am happy,' he wrote, 'and I will continue to be happy' (Philippians 1:18 [NCV]). And his message to the church at Philippi echoed the words of Jesus by the lake: 'Be full of joy in the Lord always. I will say again, be full of joy' (Philippians 4:4 [NCV])" (*Blessings,* 35–38; see also *Thoughts From the Mount of Blessing,* 31–35).

Questions to consider

1. How did Jesus face the lies of this world? How should we?

2. How do insult and persecution help spread the gospel?

3. What is the reward in this life for following God? Is there an occasion in your life when you experienced this reward?

The Salt of the Earth 8

This study is based on Matthew 5:13 and
Thoughts From the Mount of Blessing, chapter 2
—see also *Blessings,* chapter 2.

Mingle and change

As the sun rose over the horizon that morning, the world began to sparkle. The dew on the grass and leaves radiated a shiny glow. Across the face of the lake, waves broke down in shimmers that seemed to reflect the sun a million times. From every perspective it was a world made fresh, a world made new once more.

The people seated on the grass were astonished at Jesus' words. Once more, He said things they didn't expect, things they had never heard before. Speaking to them as if they were already citizens of the kingdom of heaven, He gave them not only a path to follow but a worldview they had never before imagined.

"You are the salt of the earth," He said, His arms swinging wide as if to invite their gaze. And in the distance, they did see the salt of the earth. They saw salt glistening in the morning sun along every path through the grass and hills.

Salt was an integral part of life in Jesus' day. Today, we use salt mainly as a seasoning, to melt ice or snow, or to make homemade ice cream! In those days, salt was used primarily as a preservative, a way to keep food fresh, especially meat. Without refrigerators or freezers, it was difficult to keep food from spoiling quickly.

Salt preserves because it permeates and changes what it is added to. Christians can work in the same way in society, but they must be a part of it if they are to change it. Through personal contacts and friendships, we can touch people with the gospel of Jesus. We must make friends of those we wish to reach. When they can see in us a love of life, a sense of peace when difficulties arise, and a confident view of the future, they will want to know what we know—and who we know. But like salt, we must mingle with them if we are to change them.

Salt available in the Middle East in those days was not the same purified variety we can buy today. It was harvested from swampy land and was usually thoroughly mixed with mud, soil, and organic matter. As it was used to preserve food, it tended to get more diluted with organic matter until finally the mixture didn't have enough saltiness to work as a preservative. When that happened, the mixture was thrown out onto pathways. It was salty enough to inhibit the growth of grasses in the pathways, but not salty enough to preserve food anymore.

This was the salt the crowd could see shining along the pathways. Each day from then on, when they walked those pathways, they would think how just as salt can lose its savor, a person who loses their passion for the Word of God will also be left behind.

But they also remembered that they could change the world—if they could share the love they saw in Jesus.

Reflect on the story

" 'You are the salt of the earth' (Matthew 5:13 [NCV]).

"Throughout history, salt has been valuable because of its ability to preserve food and keep it from spoiling. When Jesus called His followers 'salt,' He was teaching them that they could change the world around them by sharing their soul-saving message. God chooses people, not just to make them a part of His family, but to reach out through them to the rest of world with the message of salvation.

"God didn't choose Abraham just to increase His circle of friends; He chose Abraham to be a channel of blessing to the people of the earth. In His last prayer with His disciples before His crucifixion, Jesus said, 'For their sake, I am making myself ready to serve so that they can be ready for their service of the truth' John 17:19 [NCV]). As Christians are changed through the truth, the will, in turn. change the world and save it from complete moral decay.

"By penetrating food, salt preserves and changes it. In the same way, the gospel changes people through personal contact and friendship with God's followers. We must make friends with those we hope to help. They will respond to the gospel as individuals, not in mass groups.

"The saltiness of salt represents the true power of the Christian—the love of Jesus in the heart and the righteousness of Jesus in the life. If Jesus' love lives in our hearts, it will flow out to others. As we make friends with people, their hearts will be warmed by the unselfish kindness we show them. All sincere believers radiate a life-enhancing energy that touches and strengthens the people around them, especially those they are trying to reach with the gospel. This power is not ours, but the power of the Holy Spirit that begins to change hearts and minds" (*Blessings*, 38, 39; see also *Thoughts From the Mount of Blessing*, 35, 36).

Questions to consider

1. Why did Jesus call His followers "salt"? In what ways are Christians like salt?

2. "We must make friends with those we hope to help." What does this teach us about evangelism?

3. What does the saltiness of salt represent? Who is being touched and strengthened by your life-enhancing energy?

Reflect on the story

"As they listened to the words of Christ, the people could see the white salt glistening in the pathways where it had been cast out because it had lost its savor and was therefore useless. It well represented the condition of the Pharisees and the effect of their religion upon society. It represents the life of every soul from whom the power of the grace of God has departed and who has become cold and Christless. Whatever may be his profession, such a one is looked upon by men and angels as insipid and disagreeable. It is to such that Christ says: 'I would thou wert cold or hot. So then because thou art lukewarm, and neither cold nor hot, I will spue thee out of My mouth.' Revelation 3:15, 16.

"Without a living faith in Christ as a personal Saviour it is impossible to make our influence felt in a skeptical world. We cannot give to others that which we do not ourselves possess. It is in proportion to our own devotion and consecration to Christ that we exert an influence for the blessing and uplifting of mankind. If there is no actual service, no genuine love, no reality of experience, there is no power to help, no connection with heaven, no savor of Christ in the life. Unless the Holy Spirit can use us as agents through whom to communicate to the world the truth as it is in Jesus, we are as salt that has lost its savor and is entirely worthless. By our lack of the grace of Christ we testify to the world that the truth which we claim to believe has no sanctifying power; and thus, so far as our influence goes, we make of no effect the word of God. 'If I speak with the tongues of men and of angels, but have not love, I am become sounding brass, or a clanging cymbal. And if I have the gift of prophecy, and know all mysteries and all knowledge; and if I have all faith, so as to remove mountains, but have not love, I am nothing. And if I bestow all my goods to feed the poor, and if I give my body to be burned, but have not love, it profiteth me nothing.' 1 Corinthians 13:1-3, A.R.V.

"When love fills the heart, it will flow out to others, not because of favors received from them, but because love is the principle of action. Love modifies the character, governs the impulses, subdues enmity, and ennobles the affections. This love is as broad as the universe, and is in harmony with that of the angel workers. Cherished in the heart, it sweetens the entire life and sheds its blessing upon all around. It is this, and this only, that can make us the salt of the earth" (*Thoughts From the Mount of Blessing*, 36–38; see also *Blessings*, 39–41).

Questions to consider

1. Why was salt thrown onto the pathways in Jesus' day? How does that illustrate Christians who have lost their connection to God?

2. What are we telling the world when we claim to be Christians but show no faith, no love for others?

3. What is the only thing that can make us the "salt of the earth"? Is that seen today in our churches, our families, our daily lives?

The Light of the World   9

This study is based on Matthew 5:14, 15 and
Thoughts From the Mount of Blessing, chapter 2
—see also *Blessings,* chapter 2.

Let it shine!

As the crowd gathered that morning by the lake, the sun was beginning to climb above the horizon. As was common in all preindustrial societies, daily life in Israel began and ended with the sun. Particularly for the working people, there was no staying up late to read or party by torch or candlelight. When it got dark, they went home and went to bed. When the sky brightened, they were up and starting their day.

On this glorious morning, sunlight began to chase away the shadows of night and glimmered on the wrinkled face of the lake. Birds added their splash of color and song as they swooped down around the dew-sparkled flowers and grass. To many of the people who sat there—people who would normally have been hard at work by this hour—it must have been a wondrous and peaceful moment.

Jesus often used common, everyday things to illustrate the truths He taught. By using objects and situations they would see again and again, He knew that they would remember His words and think on them often. Knowing that this was an illustration they would be reminded of every day of their lives, He looked out into their faces, glanced toward the sun, and said, "You are the light of the world."

The light of the world! They must have stared at each other in amazement! Could they really light up the world as the sun was lighting up the sky all around them? Could they really drive out the darkness and transform others with the light?

As the people processed that thought, Jesus lifted His arms and pointed to the towns and villages on the surrounding hills. "A city on a hill cannot be hidden," He said. In those days, villages were built on hills so they could be defended in case of an attack. With only spears, swords, and arrows, attackers who had to run uphill toward a village or town were at a great disadvantage. Men with bows and arrows in the village could fire down upon the enemy easily. And even when they came within reach of their spears, those holding spears from a higher elevation usually won any contest. No one built a city on a hill to hide it from their enemies. They built it on a hill so that any enemy could see how hard it would be to attack.

The hills around them that morning were dotted with villages and towns. And each was bathed in the light of the morning sun. "No one builds a village on a hill so it won't be seen," Jesus said, "no more than they light a candle and then hide it under a basket." The purpose of lighting a candle is to spread light.

Many heads nodded in agreement at that statement. Most of the peasants and fishermen in the crowd lived in small one-room houses. When the sun went down, they could light a single candle and illuminate the whole house while the final chores or tasks were done. The idea of lighting that candle and then hiding it under a basket was ludicrous.

And that's the thought Jesus wanted them to remember, not just that day but every day when a candle was lit: If we are followers of Jesus, if we believe in God, then our faith should shine out like a beacon to all who are searching for hope and truth.

Reflect on the story

" 'Ye are the light of the world.' Matthew 5:14.

"As Jesus taught the people, He made His lessons interesting and held the attention of His hearers by frequent illustrations from the scenes of nature about them. The people had come together while it was yet morning. The glorious sun, climbing higher and higher in the blue sky, was chasing away the shadows that lurked in the valleys and among the narrow defiles of the mountains. The glory of the eastern heavens had not yet faded out. The sunlight flooded the land with its splendor; the placid surface of the lake reflected the golden light and mirrored the rosy clouds of morning. Every bud and flower and leafy spray glistened with dewdrops. Nature smiled under the benediction of a new day, and the birds sang sweetly among the trees. The Saviour looked upon the company before Him, and then to the rising sun, and said to His disciples, 'Ye are the light of the world.' As the sun goes forth on its errand of love, dispelling the shades of night and awakening the world to life, so the followers of Christ are to go forth on their mission, diffusing the light of heaven upon those who are in the darkness of error and sin.

"In the brilliant light of the morning, the towns and villages upon the surrounding hills stood forth clearly, making an attractive feature of the scene. Pointing to them, Jesus said, 'A city set on a hill cannot be hid.' And he added, 'Neither do men light a lamp, and put it under the bushel, but on the stand; and it shineth unto all that are in the house.' R.V. Most of those who listened to the words of Jesus were peasants and fishermen whose lowly dwellings contained but one room, in which the single lamp on its stand shone to all in the house. Even so, said Jesus, 'Let your light so shine before men, that they may see your good works, and glorify your Father which is in heaven.'

"No other light ever has shone or ever will shine upon fallen man save that which emanates from Christ. Jesus, the Saviour, is the only light that can illuminate the darkness of a world lying in sin. Of Christ it is written, 'In Him was life; and the life was the light of men.' John 1:4. It was by receiving of His life that His disciples could become light bearers. The life of Christ in the soul, His love revealed in the character, would make them the light of the world.

"Humanity has in itself no light. Apart from Christ we are like an unkindled taper, like the moon when her face is turned away from the sun; we have not a single ray of brightness to shed into the darkness of the world. But when we turn toward the Sun of Righteousness, when we come in touch with Christ, the whole soul is aglow with the brightness of the divine presence.

"Christ's followers are to be more than a light in the midst of men. They are *the* light of the world. Jesus says to all who have named His name, You have given yourselves to Me, and I have given you to the world as My representatives. As the Father had sent Him into the world, so, He declares, 'have I also sent them into the world.' John 17:18. As Christ is the channel for the revelation of the Father, so we are to be the channel for the revelation of Christ. While our Saviour is the great source of illumination, forget not, O Christian, that He is revealed through humanity. God's blessings are bestowed through human instrumentality. Christ Himself came to the world as the Son of man. Humanity, united to the divine nature, must touch humanity. The church of Christ, every individual disciple of the Master, is heaven's appointed channel for the revelation of God to men. Angels of glory wait to communicate through you heaven's light and power to souls that are ready to perish. Shall the human agent fail of accomplishing his appointed work? Oh, then to that degree is the world robbed of the promised influence of the Holy Spirit!

"But Jesus did not bid the disciples, 'Strive to *make* your light shine;' He said, '*Let* it shine.' If Christ is dwelling in the heart, it is impossible to conceal the light of His presence. If those who profess to be followers of Christ are not the light of the world, it is because the vital power has left them; if they have no light to give, it is because they have no connection with the Source of light" (*Thoughts From the Mount of Blessing*, 38–41; see also *Blessings*, 41–44).

Questions to consider

1. How can our lives be like the new moon? Or like when the moon is full?

2. What does it mean that God's blessings are bestowed through human instrumentality? Does that mean that those around us can lose out on God's blessings because we fail to do our part in sharing them?

3. Jesus did not bid the disciples, "Strive to *make* your light shine;" He said, "*Let* it shine." What is the difference between those two statements? What do you need to do to let your light shine?

Reflect on the story

"Throughout history, the Spirit of Christ has made God's true followers the light to the people of their day. Joseph was a light bearer in Egypt. With purity and kindness and brotherly love, he represented Christ in the middle of a culture that worshiped many gods. While the Israelites traveled from Egypt to Canaan, the faithful among them shone like a light, revealing God to the surrounding nations. From Daniel and his friends in Babylon, as well as from Mordecai in Persia, bright beams of light shone out, combating the darkness in the courts of kings.

"In the same way, Christ's disciples today must be light bearers. Through us, the Father's mercy and goodness are shown to a world darkened by a misunderstanding of God. By seeing our acts of love, others are led to God. Our lives make it clear that there is a praiseworthy God on the throne of the universe, One after whom we can pattern our lives. The glow of divine love in our hearts and the peace and harmony of Jesus in our lives are glimpses of heaven to those around us. This is the way people are led to believe that God loves them. This is how their sinful hearts are purified and transformed.

"With the words, 'You are the light of the world,' Jesus committed His followers to a worldwide mission (NIV). In Jesus' day, selfishness, pride, and prejudice had built a wall between the Jews—the guardians of God's truth—and the rest of the world. But Jesus came to change that. The words people heard from His lips were not like anything they had ever heard from the priests or rabbis. Jesus tore down that selfish wall of prejudice and taught that we should love everyone, everywhere. His love lifts people out of their small selfish circles and abolishes national and social distinctions. Jesus sees no difference between neighbors and strangers or friends and enemies. He teaches us to see every person in need as a neighbor and to see the world as our neighborhood.

"Just as the rays of the sun reach the farthest edges of the earth, God wants the light of the gospel to reach every person in the world. If God's church was living up to His plan, the light would reach everyone who sits in darkness. Instead of meeting together each week in comfort and forgetting their mission, church members would scatter out into the nations, letting their light shine and carrying the gospel to all the world.

"This is the way that God's plan to gather followers has always been fulfilled—from Abraham on the plains of Mesopotamia to our day. God says, 'I will bless you. . . . And you will be a blessing to others' (Genesis 12:2 [NCV]). If the glory of God has touched your heart, if you have seen the beauty of His love, then Jesus is speaking to you. Have your felt God's life-changing power? Then many others who are addicted to sin and sorrow are waiting to hear your words of faith.

"We can't be satisfied just to know about God's love and power. We must share what we know with others. The prophet Isaiah and King David both saw the glorious love of God and then shared their response in poetry and song. Who can see Jesus' glory and His plan to save men and women—and not share it with others? Who could be touched by the incomprehensible love Jesus showed on the cross to save us—and not praise God to everyone who will listen?

"The writer of the Psalms praised God with a song, saying, 'Parents will tell their children what you have done. They will retell your mighty acts, wonderful majesty, and glory. And I will think about your miracles. They will tell about the amazing things you do, and I will tell how great you are' (Psalm 145:4–6 [NCV]).

"Whenever the story of the Cross is told, it captures people's minds and focuses their thoughts. Then their spiritual senses are charged with divine power, and their energy can be concentrated on God's work. These workers will brighten the earth like beams of light.

"Jesus gladly accepts the efforts of every person who follows Him. Through Him, humanity combines with the divinity, and the mysteries of God's gift of love are explained. We can talk about that love, pray about it, sing about it, and broadcast it all over the earth.

"The light of God's love shines brightly in contrast to the dark and selfish heart. That light shines when we handle troubles patiently, when we receive blessings gratefully, when we resist temptation, when we show humility, kindness, mercy, and love every day in everything we do" (*Blessings,* 44–46; see also *Thoughts From the Mount of Blessing,* 41–44).

Questions to consider

1. How were God's followers a light to their world in their day? How can we be light bearers today? How can you be a light bearer in your community?

2. How can we "see every person in need as a neighbor and . . . the world as our neighborhood"? Are there people in the world we don't want in our neighborhood? What should we do?

3. If the glory of God has touched your heart, if you have seen the beauty of His love, then Jesus is speaking to you. Have you felt God's life-changing power? Who in your life is waiting to hear your words of faith?

4. What do you have to share when you think of Jesus' love for you on the cross?

Keeping the Law 10

This study is based on Matthew 5:17, 18 and
Thoughts From the Mount of Blessing, chapter 3
—see also *Blessings,* chapter 3.

Who a person should be

This was not the first time Jesus had met a crowd of His people on a mountainside. In the days of Moses, Jesus met His people at Sinai. The setting there was very different—fire swept the top of the mountain, dark clouds swirled through the sky, and the ground shook as earthquakes rattled the structure of the mountain itself.

At Sinai, the people fell on their faces, terrified by the display of power. As God's voice rolled through the crags and crevices, the people quaked as badly as the mountain. There they listened as God's law thundered across the hills. They swore to obey it. But through so much of their history, their religious leaders focused on obeying the rituals and following the rules instead of allowing their hearts to be changed.

But on this day, in the bright sunshine, Jesus again explained the principles of the law that He had thundered on Sinai. This time He used a quieter voice, explained them as principles of His kingdom, and invited each person to become a citizen of that kingdom.

But as they had through history, the Jewish leaders and Pharisees present that day were focused on rituals and rules. They didn't understand the idea of a changed heart. Following the rules was hard work, but they were willing to do it in order to be considered holy. That was their understanding of righteousness—doing the right things in public where everyone could see. Nothing else mattered.

With that attitude, the Jewish leaders didn't understand or accept Jesus's teachings. And they were certain that He didn't insist nearly enough about the importance of keeping the law. Jesus tried to explain the truths on which the rules were based, but they accused Him of saying that God's law didn't need to be kept. In their hearts, they were sure that Jesus would have to be killed in order to protect God's law.

As strange as that sounds to us, their reasoning followed a certain logic. If Jesus continued to teach that keeping God's law wasn't important, and the people continued to listen, many would begin behaving like Jesus did. With no respect for God's law, their country would lose the protection of God. Those with no respect for God's law would certainly not respect the laws of the Romans. This would lead to an open, armed rebellion against Rome. Without God's special protection, the country of Israel would be completely destroyed. It was better for one person—Jesus—to die than for the whole country to be destroyed.

It is odd that both Jesus and the Pharisees thought He needed to die in order to uphold God's law. But unlike the Pharisees, Jesus was motivated by self-sacrificing love and a clear understanding of what it meant to truly keep the law of God.

Everything in the universe obeys laws. From the mote of dust in a sunbeam to the orbit of Phobos around the planet Mars—everything does just as the laws of gravity and motion demand. Laws govern the natural world, and everything that lives obeys them. In the same way, laws of righteousness govern the way intelligent beings should live. It is possible for an intelligent being to break those laws—for a time. Because of God's grace and Jesus' sacrifice, the penalty for breaking the laws of righteousness has been held off temporarily.

But make no mistake. Breaking the laws of life and love can only result in death. God's universe was not created to tolerate hate and cruelty and sin. It is a place designed to allow peace and happiness to exist forever, to allow joy to last forever.

Everything Jesus taught was in support of the law. He didn't talk so much about what a person should do or not do—He focused on who a person should be or not be. And a person who wishes to be a part of God's kingdom should be a person like Jesus.

Reflect on the story

> " 'I have not come to destroy them [God's commandments] but to bring
> about what they said' (Matthew 5:17 [NCV]).

"It was Jesus Himself, with thunder and fire, who had announced the Ten Commandments on Mount Sinai. Like a ravenous fire, God's glory engulfed the mountain peak, and His presence made the mountain quake. The people of Israel flung themselves flat on their faces, listening in awe to the holy principles of the law.

"How different it was centuries later when Jesus spoke on the hillside by the lake! Under a summer sky with nothing but the songs of birds to break the silence, Jesus lovingly explained the principles of His kingdom—the same principles of the law He had earlier announced on Sinai.

"When the law was given at Sinai, the Israelites had just escaped generations of slavery in Egypt. They needed to be impressed with God's power and majesty. But He also showed them that He is a God of love. 'The LORD came from Mount Sinai and rose like the sun from Edom; he showed his greatness from Mount Paran. He came with thousands of angels from the southern mountains. The LORD surely loves his people and takes care of all those who belong to him. They bow down at his feet, and they are taught by him' (Deuteronomy 33:2, 3 [NCV]).

"And God described Himself to Moses in words long treasured by believers: 'I am the LORD. The LORD is a God who shows mercy, who is kind, who doesn't become angry quickly, who has great love and faithfulness and is kind to thousands of people. The LORD forgives people for evil, for sin, and for turning against him, but he does not forget to punish guilty people' (Exodus 34:6, 7 [NCV]).

"The law Jesus gave on Sinai expressed principles of love, and revealed the law of heaven to earth. The One who spoke the words of the law was the very One who would later come to earth and provide the power to live in harmony with those laws. And God made it very clear why He was giving His law to the Israelites: 'You are to be my holy people' (Exodus 22:31 [NCV]).

"But the Israelites didn't understand the spiritual nature of the law. Instead, they focused on performing the rituals and obeying the rules instead of allowing their hearts to be changed by love.

In everything He said and did, Jesus communicated the kind, generous, fatherly love of God and the pointlessness of blindly performing rituals and following rules. But the Jewish leaders didn't understand or accept His teachings. They didn't think He emphasized strongly enough the importance of keeping the law. When He explained the actual truths on which their rituals and rules were based, they accused Him of plotting to do away with God's law.

"As Jesus spoke to the people on the mountainside about God's law, He spoke calmly, but with such power and conviction that their hearts were touched. They were accustomed to the rabbis lifelessly reciting rules, so Jesus' words shocked them. They 'were amazed at his teaching, because he did not teach like their teachers of the law. He taught like a person who had authority' (Matthew 7:28, 29 [NCV]).

"The Pharisees could see the difference in Jesus' teaching style also. And they could see that His explanation of the power and beauty of truth—so simple yet so deep—was captivating the people. They could see that His gentle, loving manner was opening the people's hearts. It was clear to them that Jesus' teaching was destroying everything they had taught and worked for. He was tearing down the walls that gave them their proud, exclusive status. They were afraid that if they didn't do something, Jesus would turn everyone completely against them. So they followed Him, watching for some way to discredit Him in front of the crowds and thus pave the way to have Him arrested and killed" (*Blessings,* 47–49; see also *Thoughts From the Mount of Blessing,* 45–47).

Questions to consider

1. Why did God need to use power and majesty on Mount Sinai? Are there times today when He needs to do the same?

2. How did the Israelites fail to understand the spiritual nature of the law? Are we in danger of doing the same today?

3. How was Jesus' teaching different than that of the Pharisees? What should that teach us about how we present God's truths to others?

Reflect on the story

"On the mount, Jesus was closely watched by spies; and as He unfolded the principles of righteousness, the Pharisees caused it to be whispered about that His teaching was in opposition to the precepts that God had given from Sinai. The Saviour said nothing to unsettle faith in the religion and institutions that had been given through Moses; for every ray of divine light that Israel's great leader communicated to his people was received from Christ. While many are saying in their hearts that He has come to do away with the law, Jesus in unmistakable language reveals His attitude toward the divine statutes. 'Think not,' He said, 'that I am come to destroy the law, or the prophets.'

"It is the Creator of men, the Giver of the law, who declares that it is not His purpose to set aside its precepts. Everything in nature, from the mote in the sunbeam to the worlds on high, is under law. And upon obedience to these laws the order and harmony of the natural world depend. So there are great principles of righteousness to control the life of all intelligent beings, and upon conformity to these principles the well-being of the universe depends. Before this earth was called into being, God's law existed. Angels are governed by its principles, and in order for earth to be in harmony with heaven, man also must obey the divine statutes. To man in Eden Christ made known the precepts of the law 'when the morning stars sang together, and all the sons of God shouted for joy.' Job 38:7. The mission of Christ on earth was not to destroy the law, but by His grace to bring man back to obedience to its precepts.

"The beloved disciple, who listened to the words of Jesus on the mount, writing long afterward under the inspiration of the Holy Spirit, speaks of the law as of perpetual obligation. He says that 'sin is the transgression of the law' and that 'whosoever committeth sin transgresseth also the law.' 1 John 3:4. He makes it plain that the law to which he refers is 'an old commandment which ye had from the beginning.' 1 John 2:7. He is speaking of the law that existed at the creation and was reiterated upon Mount Sinai.

"Speaking of the law, Jesus said, 'I am not come to destroy, but to fulfill.' He here used the word 'fulfill' in the same sense as when He declared to John the Baptist His purpose to 'fulfill all righteousness' (Matthew 3:15); that is, to fill up the measure of the law's requirement, to give an example of perfect conformity to the will of God.

"His mission was to 'magnify the law, and make it honorable.' Isaiah 42:21. He was to show the spiritual nature of the law, to present its far-reaching principles, and to make plain its eternal obligation.

"The divine beauty of the character of Christ, of whom the noblest and most gentle among men are but a faint reflection; of whom Solomon by the Spirit of inspiration wrote, He is 'the chiefest among ten thousand, . . . yea, He is altogether lovely' (Song of Solomon 5:10-16); of whom David, seeing Him in prophetic vision, said, 'Thou art fairer than the children of men' (Psalm 45:2); Jesus, the express image of the Father's person, the effulgence of His glory; the self-denying Redeemer, throughout His pilgrimage of love on earth, was a living representation of the character of the law of God. In His life it is made manifest that heaven-born love, Christlike principles, underlie the laws of eternal rectitude.

" 'Till heaven and earth pass,' said Jesus, 'one jot or one tittle shall in nowise pass from the law, till all be fulfilled.' By His own obedience to the law, Christ testified to its immutable character and proved that through His grace it could be perfectly obeyed by every son and daughter of Adam. On the mount He declared that not the smallest iota should pass from the law till all things should be accomplished—all things that concern the human race, all that relates to the plan of redemption. He does not teach that the law is ever to be abrogated, but He fixes the eye upon the utmost verge of man's horizon and assures us that until this point is reached the law will retain its authority so that none may suppose it was His mission to abolish the precepts of the law. So long as heaven and earth continue, the holy principles of God's law will remain. His righteousness, 'like the great mountains' (Psalm 36:6), will continue, a source of blessing, sending forth streams to refresh the earth" (*Thoughts From the Mount of Blessing*, 47–50; see also *Blessings*, 49–52).

Questions to consider

1. How can we know that Jesus did not go against the teachings of Moses?

2. The Pharisees accused Jesus of trying to do away with the law. How do we know that He wasn't doing that? How does His example show the importance of the law?

The Kingdom of Heaven 11

This study is based on Matthew 5:19, 20 and
Thoughts From the Mount of Blessing, chapter 3
—see also *Blessings,* chapter 3.

Religion based on love

It had been a confusing morning for the disciples. Early, before they met the crowd, they had spent some quality time with Jesus. They didn't realize it, but He had been praying for them through the night. His time was growing short and with their limited education and long years of listening to the Pharisees, they had much to learn.

That morning, before the sun rose, Jesus gathered them into a circle around Him. As He spoke of the work they would do, and encouraged them to do it faithfully, He placed His hands on each of their heads in turn. He prayed and blessed them, asking His Father to give them understanding. He asked His Father to give them courage to light the world with His message and His love. In doing this, Jesus dedicated each of His disciples to the work of sharing His gospel that day and every day for the rest of their lives.

Then they left the quiet spot where they had slept and prayed and walked down to the lakeshore where the crowd was already gathering. Among the peasants, fishermen, and merchants were the scribes and Pharisees—the religious leaders of their country.

Looking out into their eyes, the disciples were confused. These Jewish leaders accused Jesus and the disciples of being sinners because they ignored so many of the rituals and ceremonies that the rabbis said were required by God. They had spent their whole lives trying to live up to what the Pharisees demanded. But now Jesus said that their demands were not important. Was Jesus wrong? Or were the Pharisees wrong?

Throughout the years, the Jewish nation had claimed to be God's chosen people. But everything Jesus said showed that their religion had no saving faith. These leaders had perfected their way of living by outwardly not breaking any of the laws they proclaimed to be of importance, but there was nothing inside of them. Their hearts held no kindness, no love for others. They were not like Jesus at all.

Any religion based solely on keeping laws or acting "right" is not a religion that brings a person closer to God. Without love and kindness, it actually keeps people away. The only belief system that changes a person's life, that can transform a person's character, is a religion based on love.

What Jesus was explaining that morning was what religion actually looks like when you follow God. He was trying to explain the lifestyle that He lived—caring for others and following God faithfully.

Both the Pharisees and the disciples should have remembered what Jesus had taught through the Old Testament prophets. Jesus' teachings weren't new—they were a part of the message the prophets faithfully had recorded. Micah said, "What does God ask of you? To act fairly, to show kindness, to be humble before God" (adapted from Micah 6:8).

Reflect on the story

> " 'Whosoever . . . shall break one of these least commandments, and
> shall teach men so, he shall be called the least in the kingdom of heaven.'
> Matthew 5:19.

"That is, he shall have no place therein. For he who willfully breaks one commandment, does not, in spirit and truth, keep any of them. 'Whosoever shall keep the whole law, and yet offend in one point, he is guilty of all.' James 2:10.

"It is not the greatness of the act of disobedience that constitutes sin, but the fact of variance from God's expressed will in the least particular; for this shows that there is yet communion between the soul and sin. The heart is divided in its service. There is a virtual denial of God, a rebellion against the laws of His government.

"Were men free to depart from the Lord's requirements and to set up a standard of duty for themselves, there would be a variety of standards to suit different minds and the government would be taken out of the Lord's hands. The will of man would be made supreme, and the high and holy will of God—His purpose of love toward His creatures—would be dishonored, disrespected.

"Whenever men choose their own way, they place themselves in controversy with God. They will have no place in the kingdom of heaven, for they are at war with the very principles of heaven. In disregarding the will of God, they are placing themselves on the side of Satan, the enemy of God and man. Not by one word, not by many words, but by every word that God has spoken, shall man live. We cannot disregard one word, however trifling it may seem to us, and be safe. There is not a commandment of the law that is not for the good and happiness of man, both in this life and in the life to come. In obedience to God's law, man is surrounded as with a hedge and kept from the evil. He who breaks down this divinely erected barrier at one point has destroyed its power to protect him; for he has opened a way by which the enemy can enter to waste and ruin.

"By venturing to disregard the will of God upon one point, our first parents opened the floodgates of woe upon the world. And every individual who follows their example will reap a similar result. The love of God underlies every precept of His law, and he who departs from the commandment is working his own unhappiness and ruin" (*Thoughts From the Mount of Blessing*, 51, 52; see also *Blessings*, 52, 53).

Questions to consider

1. What is it that constitutes sin? Why is it that breaking one commandment makes a person guilty of breaking all of them?

2. How is God's law a hedge that protects us from evil? What is the result of disregarding the will of God in any small way?

Reflect on the story

> " 'I tell you that if you are no more obedient than the teachers of the law and the Pharisees, you will never enter the kingdom of heaven'
> (Matthew 5:20 [NCV]).

"The Jewish leaders accused Jesus and His disciples of being sinners because they ignored the rituals and ceremonies of the rabbis. This confused the disciples. They were accustomed to listening to and honoring these religious leaders. But Jesus exposed their religion and self-righteousness as worthless. The Jewish nation claimed to be God's chosen people, but Jesus showed that their religion had no saving faith. All their attempts to appear righteous, all their rituals and ceremonies, all their claims of living without breaking God's law, did not make them holy. Their hearts were not pure; they were not kind and just; they were not like Jesus.

"A religion based on keeping laws or rules doesn't bring a person into harmony with God. The Pharisees' hard, rigid belief system showed no kindness, forgiveness, or love; it was actually a barrier to sinners. It kept people away from God. Like salt that has lost its saltiness, the beliefs of the Jewish leaders did nothing to save the world from spoiling with sin. The only true religion is the one that works to change people's hearts with love. That kind of religion can transform a person's character.

"The Jewish people should have learned all this from the teachings of the prophets. Hundreds of years earlier, the prophet Micah had addressed the same issue: 'You say, "What can I bring with me when I come before the LORD, when I bow before God on high? Should I come before him with burnt offerings, with year-old calves? Will the LORD be pleased with a thousand male sheep? Will he be pleased with ten thousand rivers of oil?" . . . The LORD has told you, human, what is good; he has told you what he wants from you: to do what is right to other people, love being kind to others, and live humbly, obeying your God' (Micah 6:6–8 [NCV]).

"The prophet Hosea compared the Pharisees' type of religion to an empty vine that produces fruit only for itself. Their righteousness of the Jewish leaders was the 'fruit' of their own efforts to keep the law according to their own ideas and for their own selfish benefit. Clearly, their righteousness could be no better than they were themselves. In trying to make themselves holy, they were trying to make a 'clean' thing out of an 'unclean' thing. God's law is as holy and perfect as He is. It shows humans what God's righteousness is like. Human nature is twisted and selfish, so it's impossible for human beings, by their own power, to keep God's law. The actions of a selfish heart are dirty with sin and 'all the right things we have done are like filthy pieces of cloth' (Isaiah 64:6 [NCV]).

"The law is holy, but the Jews could not become holy by trying to keep it. So the followers of Jesus had to look for something different from what the Pharisees taught if they wanted to enter the kingdom of heaven. God gave them His Son, whose life was a perfect reflection of the law. If they would open their hearts and accept Jesus, then God would live in them and His love would transform them into someone like Him. God would give them the righteousness that the law demands. But the Pharisees rejected Jesus. They were intent on earning their own righteousness and would not stoop to learn about the righteousness of God.

"Jesus showed those who listened to Him what it means to keep the commandments—it means reflecting His character in their own lives and actions" (*Blessings*, 54–56; see also *Thoughts From the Mount of Blessing*, 53–55).

Questions to consider

1. The Pharisees and Jewish leaders appeared to the disciples to be righteous and holy. Why did the disciples think this was so? Could it be that we are also fooled into thinking that certain people are righteous? Who and why?

2. Why was the Pharisees' belief system a barrier to sinners? What can we do to be sure that we are not such a barrier?

3. The followers of Jesus needed something different than what the Pharisees had. In spite of what we may have learned about the importance of keeping the commandments, what do we need in order to keep them?

No Room for Hate 12

This study is based on Matthew 5:22–24 and
Thoughts From the Mount of Blessing, chapter 3
—see also *Blessings,* chapter 3.

Life without baggage

Many of those on the hillside that morning had heard Jesus speak before. The disciples, of course, were His constant companions along the roads and through the towns. The Pharisee spies were almost as faithful to be wherever He might attract a crowd. They wanted to know what He was saying so they could find a way to use it against Him when the time was right. Also, by being there they had opportunities to explain to the people how mistaken Jesus was.

Besides these, a crowd of people followed wherever Jesus went. They wanted to witness a crippled man take his first strong steps. They wanted to hear the first shouts of the previously mute woman. They wanted to gasp in astonishment at the leper's new clean skin. And you never knew when Jesus might miraculously provide bread and fish for everyone's lunch.

Jesus was the biggest show in town! There was always excitement in the air wherever He went.

Of course, all of these people heard Jesus' words each day as well. His description of a God of love amazed them. His explanation of the kingdom of heaven was new and confusing. Eventually, many of these people would become followers and help take the gospel to the world. But for now, they mostly followed Jesus for the entertainment—and the possibility that He would announce Himself as King and lead them to drive out the hated Romans.

If there was one thing the people in the crowd that morning had in common, it was their hatred for the Romans. Since the Roman Empire had moved in to control Israel in 63 B.C., the Jewish people had suffered under their rule. One of the greatest hopes of the people was that the long-promised Messiah would come and free them. Many followed Jesus hoping that He would be the One.

But Jesus wasn't there to fight through military force or politics. Instead, He fought against hatred—hatred of any kind.

There was plenty of hatred and animosity just among the people in the crowd. The peasants hated the Pharisees for their "holier than thou" attitude. The Pharisees hated the peasants for not living according to the strict rules they found so important. And so many hated anyone else who didn't believe and behave the same way they did.

To these people, Jesus introduced a new concept. "Don't hate. Hate is the seed of murder in your heart." Even though the prophets had taught that you should love your neighbor as yourself, that teaching had been lost to the Jewish people. Jesus taught it again, and the people were astonished at the teaching.

Jesus was teaching that how you treat one another as Christians—as humans—matters a great deal. A believer cannot treat others cruelly and still say they are following Jesus. A believer cannot be mean and still say they are part of the kingdom of heaven.

Has someone been mean to you? Then forgive them. Revenge is a seed of hate in your heart that will grow until you are no longer connected to God at all. Hatred—even if justified by human standards—is only a path to more pain, to less love, and to less happiness.

Revenge, hatred, meanness are all vines that will tie you down so that you cannot escape. Being a follower of Jesus gives you the ability to forgive those who offend you or hurt you, and by forgiving, you are able to go on with your life without that baggage. You are able to be happy because you are not carrying their pain.

And it is true that we can make it right when we hurt someone. We can ask forgiveness and make restitution if needed. When we do so, we preserve our ability to be happy, to have the life that Jesus promised, and to become citizens of the kingdom of heaven.

Reflect on the story

> *" 'But I tell you, if you are angry with a brother or sister, you will be judged' (Matthew 5:22 [NCV]).*

"Through the prophet Moses, God had said, ' "You must not hate your fellow citizen in your heart. . . . Forget about the wrong things people do to you, and do not try to get even. Love your neighbor as you love yourself" ' (Leviticus 19:17, 18 [NCV]). Jesus' teachings had been taught by the prophets long before, but they had become hidden because of hard hearts and the love of sin. Jesus' words made it clear to His listeners that when they condemned others for sinning, their meanness and hate made them just as guilty as the ones they condemned.

"Across the lake from the spot where Jesus was preaching that morning was the region called Bashan, a remote area of wild canyons and forests that was a favorite hiding place for criminals of all kinds. Everyone listening to Jesus had heard recent reports of robberies and murders committed there, and many were quick to condemn these evil people. But at the same time, they themselves were hotheaded and contrary. They felt bitter hatred for the Romans who ruled them, and they felt free to hate and despise anyone else, even other Jews who didn't do and believe everything the way they did. So they were clearly breaking the spirit of the commandment, 'You must not murder anyone.'

"The spirit of hate and revenge started with Satan, and it led him to kill the Son of God. Anyone who enjoys cruelty or meanness is embracing the same spirit, and it will lead to pain and death. Just as a plant lies dormant within a seed, an evil act lies within every thought of revenge. 'Everyone who hates a brother or sister is a murderer, and you know that no murderers have eternal life in them' (1 John 3:15 [NCV]).

" 'If you say bad things to a brother or sister, you will be judged by the council' (Matthew 5:22 [NCV]). By giving His own Son to save us, God shows how highly He values every human soul, and He gives no one permission to harshly criticize or insult another person. We may see the faults and weaknesses of those around us, but God considers each person to be His property—His, because He is their Creator, and doubly His, because He paid for their salvation with the blood of Christ. Every human being has been created in His image, and even the most pitiful ones should be treated with respect and kindness. God will hold us responsible for every cruel and critical word spoken about a person for whom Jesus gave His life. Besides, 'Who says you are better than others? What do you have that was not given to you? And if it was given to you, why do you brag as if you did not receive it as a gift?' (1 Corinthians 4:7 [NCV]).

" 'And if you call someone a fool, you will be in danger of the fire of hell' (Matthew 5:22 [NCV]). In the Old Testament, the word *fool* is used to describe someone who has given up his faith and turned to a life of wickedness. Here Jesus says that anyone who condemns someone else as an enemy of God has earned the same condemnation.

"When Jesus fought with Satan over the body of Moses, He did not accuse or condemn him. If He had, He would have stooped to Satan's own level, because accusation is one of Satan's weapons. Jesus said only, 'The Lord punish you' (Jude 9 [NCV]).

"Jesus sets this example for us. When we argue with or struggle against the enemies of Christ, we shouldn't speak in a spirit of retaliation or accuse them of anything. Someone who speaks for God shouldn't use words that Jesus Himself wouldn't use even against Satan. We must leave all the judging and condemning to God" (*Blessings*, 56–58; see also *Thoughts From the Mount of Blessing*, 55–58).

Questions to consider

1. Does our meanness and hate make us guilty every time we condemn others for sinning? How do we speak out against sin without condemning sinners?

2. "Someone who speaks for God shouldn't use words that Jesus Himself wouldn't use even against Satan." What words do we use that Jesus wouldn't use? Should we be more careful with what we say about others?

Reflect on the story

" 'Be reconciled to thy brother.' Matthew 5:24.

"The love of God is something more than a mere negation; it is a positive and active principle, a living spring, ever flowing to bless others. If the love of Christ dwells in us, we shall not only cherish no hatred toward our fellows, but we shall seek in every way to manifest love toward them.

"Jesus said, 'If thou bring thy gift to the altar, and there rememberest that thy brother hath aught against thee; leave there thy gift before the altar, and go thy way; first be reconciled to thy brother, and then come and offer thy gift.' The sacrificial offerings expressed faith that through Christ the offerer had become a partaker of the mercy and love of God. But for one to express faith in God's pardoning love, while he himself indulged an unloving spirit, would be a mere farce.

"When one who professes to serve God wrongs or injures a brother, he misrepresents the character of God to that brother, and the wrong must be confessed, he must acknowledge it to be sin, in order to be in harmony with God. Our brother may have done us a greater wrong than we have done him, but this does not lessen our responsibility. If when we come before God we remember that another has aught against us, we are to leave our gift of prayer, of thanksgiving, of freewill offering, and go to the brother with whom we are at variance, and in humility confess our own sin and ask to be forgiven.

"If we have in any manner defrauded or injured our brother, we should make restitution. If we have unwittingly borne false witness, if we have misstated his words, if we have injured his influence in any way, we should go to the ones with whom we have conversed about him, and take back all our injurious misstatements.

"If matters of difficulty between brethren were not laid open before others, but frankly spoken of between themselves in the spirit of Christian love, how much evil might be prevented! How many roots of bitterness whereby many are defiled would be destroyed, and how closely and tenderly might the followers of Christ be united in His love!" (*Thoughts From the Mount of Blessing,* 58, 59; see also *Blessings,* 58, 59).

Questions to consider

1. If the love of God dwells in us, how does that impact how we treat others? How often do we do this?

2. When a person who professes to serve God wrongs a brother or sister, what is the result? What should that person do?

3. If issues between people were handled privately between the individuals involved, how would evil be prevented? Can you think of a situation where private handling of misunderstandings would have prevented much hurt?

Look to Your Own Heart   13

This study is based on Matthew 5:25–30 and
Thoughts From the Mount of Blessing, chapter 3
—see also *Blessings,* chapter 3.

It's all in the heart

It was common among the Jewish people to view religion as a list of things not to do—don't walk any farther than a certain distance on the Sabbath day; don't do anything that might make you unclean and unable to go to the temple; don't associate with the wrong people or you may be condemned along with them, and much more.

Too often we see this same attitude among believers today. If you ask an Adventist what they believe, you perhaps might hear, "We don't smoke, we don't drink, we don't eat meat, we don't do anything fun on Saturday," or some such list of things we don't do. You hear far less about things that we do—things that make a difference in our families and communities.

How different it would be to live as if God's love was an active thing, always reaching out to help others, always trying to make a difference! Christianity is not about not hating others; it's about being kind to everyone.

That morning by the lake, the people could see Roman pleasure boats being readied to sail. Too often the sounds of these revelers echoed across the water as the heathen Romans pursued their sensual pleasures. This offended the Jewish people, because they felt pride in their morality. They felt that they were better than the heathen foreigners who lived only for pleasure. The Romans in particular had brought in their practice of lovers and wild parties. On the lake, in the streets, it seemed that everywhere the Jews looked, lust and sinfulness could be seen.

The crowd looked to Jesus to condemn those heathen sinners and praise the superior Jewish morality. But, as usual, Jesus pointed to the people's hearts.

"Just as thoughts of hatred are as bad as murder, thoughts of lust and adultery in the heart are as bad as the act itself," He said. What you imagine in your own heart and mind, Jesus made clear, is what you would do if you had the chance to get away with it. This means that you are no better than those who actually live an immoral life. You may not be openly sinning, but it's only because you haven't had the opportunity.

Once again, it was the heart that Jesus focused on. Here again, Jesus taught that what we need is not a stricter lifestyle, or more rules to follow. What we need is a new heart—a heart like His.

Through the prophet Ezekiel, God promised, "I will give you a new heart and put a new spirit in you; I will remove from you your heart of stone and give you a heart of flesh" (Ezekiel 36:26, NIV). It's this new heart that we are in need of.

There by the lake that morning, Jesus was trying to show them that it wasn't the strict rules of the Pharisees they needed, nor was it the loose Roman lifestyle that would make them genuinely happy. The kingdom of heaven He invited them to join didn't require a new oath of allegiance or a new passport. It required a new heart.

He offers us the same invitation today. We don't need a new commitment to Sabbath keeping or to Bible study. We don't need more hours of community service or longer sessions of prayer on our knees.

We need a new heart. And Jesus offers that gift to us today.

Reflect on the story

" 'Go and make peace with that person' (Matthew 5:24 [NCV]).

[This section is a repeat of the last reading from Thoughts From the Mount of Blessing, *but there are so many worthwhile thoughts here that it bears going through a second time.]*

"God's love is not a list of things to avoid doing. God's love is positive and active, a living spring of water always flowing to bless others. If that love lives in our hearts, we will do more than just not hate others; we will search for ways to show love and kindness to them.

"Jesus said, 'So when you offer your gift to God at the altar, and you remember that your brother or sister has something against you, leave your gift there at the altar. Go and make peace with that person, and then come and offer your gift' (Matthew 5:23, 24 [NCV]). The offerings the Jews brought to God expressed their faith that through the Messiah, they would receive mercy and love from God. But it would be a sham to express faith in a God of love and forgiveness while holding on to anger or hate for someone.

"When someone who claims to follow God offends or hurts another person, he or she misrepresents God to that person. This must be made right by confessing it as sin. Even if the other person has done more to hurt us than we have done to them, we are still responsible for our part. When we come to God in prayer or to give an offering, if we remember something we have said or done to hurt another person, we should go at once to confess and ask forgiveness.

"If we have done anything to cheat, trick, or financially injure someone, we should compensate him or her for the damage we have done. If we have misquoted someone or twisted his words to imply a different meaning or injured someone's reputation in any way, we should go to the ones we spoke to and retract our damaging words.

"If disagreements between fellow believers were not made a public matter, but worked out between them in a spirit of Christian love, much evil and negative publicity could be prevented. If Jesus' followers were tied together by His love, the bitterness that afflicts so many could be erased" (*Blessings,* 58, 59; see also *Thoughts From the Mount of Blessing,* 58, 59).

Questions to consider

1. "God's love is not a list of things to avoid doing." What is God's love then? How does it mean we relate to others?

2. If it is a sham to claim faith in God while holding on to anger and forgiveness, how often are we trapped in a sham? How do we let go of anger and forgive?

3. What would your church be like if all the bitterness could be erased? Your family?

Reflect on the story

> " 'Whosoever looketh on a woman to lust after her hath committed adultery with her already in his heart.' Matthew 5:28.

"The Jews prided themselves on their morality and looked with horror upon the sensual practices of the heathen. The presence of the Roman officers whom the imperial rule had brought into Palestine was a continual offense to the people, for with these foreigners had come in a flood of heathen customs, lust, and dissipation. In Capernaum, Roman officials with their gay paramours haunted the parades and promenades, and often the sound of revelry broke upon the stillness of the lake as their pleasure boats glided over the quiet waters. The people expected to hear from Jesus a stern denunciation of this class, but what was their astonishment as they listened to words that laid bare the evil of their own hearts!

"When the thought of evil is loved and cherished, however secretly, said Jesus, it shows that sin still reigns in the heart. The soul is still in the gall of bitterness and in the bond of iniquity. He who finds pleasure in dwelling upon scenes of impurity, who indulges the evil thought, the lustful look, may behold in the open sin, with its burden of shame and heart-breaking grief, the true nature of the evil which he has hidden in the chambers of the soul. The season of temptation, under which, it may be, one falls into grievous sin, does not create the evil that is revealed, but only develops or makes manifest that which was hidden and latent in the heart. As a man 'thinketh in his heart, so is he;' for out of the heart 'are the issues of life.' Proverbs 23:7; 4:23.

" 'If thy right hand causeth thee to stumble, cut it off, and cast it from thee.' Matthew 5:30, R.V.

"To prevent disease from spreading to the body and destroying life, a man would submit to part even with his right hand. Much more should he be willing to surrender that which imperils the life of the soul.

"Through the gospel, souls that are degraded and enslaved by Satan are to be redeemed to share the glorious liberty of the sons of God. God's purpose is not merely to deliver from the suffering that is the inevitable result of sin, but to save from sin itself. The soul, corrupted and deformed, is to be purified, transformed, that it may be clothed in 'the beauty of the Lord our God,' 'conformed to the image of His Son.' 'Eye hath not seen, nor ear heard, neither have entered into the heart of man, the things which God hath prepared for them that love Him.' Psalm 90:17; Romans 8:29; 1 Corinthians 2:9. Eternity alone can reveal the glorious destiny to which man, restored to God's image, may attain.

"In order for us to reach this high ideal, that which causes the soul to stumble must be sacrificed. It is through the will that sin retains its hold upon us. The surrender of the will is represented as plucking out the eye or cutting off the hand. Often it seems to us that to surrender the will to God is to consent to go through life maimed or crippled. But it is better, says Christ, for self to be maimed, wounded, crippled, if thus you may enter into life. That which you look upon as disaster is the door to highest benefit.

"God is the fountain of life, and we can have life only as we are in communion with Him. Separated from God, existence may be ours for a little time, but we do not possess life. 'She that liveth in pleasure is dead while she liveth.' 1 Timothy 5:6. Only through the surrender of our will to God is it possible for Him to impart life to us. Only by receiving His life through self-surrender is it possible, said Jesus, for these hidden sins, which I have pointed out, to be overcome. It is possible that you may bury them in your hearts and conceal them from human eyes, but how will you stand in God's presence?

"If you cling to self, refusing to yield your will to God, you are choosing death. To sin, wherever found, God is a consuming fire. If you choose sin, and refuse to separate from it, the presence of God, which consumes sin, must consume you.

"It will require a sacrifice to give yourself to God; but it is a sacrifice of the lower for the higher, the earthly for the spiritual, the perishable for the eternal. God does not design that our will should be destroyed, for it is only through its exercise that we can accomplish what He would have us do. Our will is to be yielded to Him, that we may receive it again, purified and refined, and so linked in sympathy with the Divine that He can pour through us the tides of His love and power. However bitter and painful this surrender may appear to the willful, wayward heart, yet 'it is profitable for thee.'

"Not until he fell crippled and helpless upon the breast of the covenant angel did Jacob know the victory of conquering faith and receive the title of a prince with God. It was when he 'halted upon his thigh' (Genesis 32:31) that the armed bands of Esau were stilled before him, and the Pharaoh, proud heir of a kingly line, stooped to crave his blessing. So the Captain of our salvation was made 'perfect through sufferings' (Hebrews 2:10), and the children of faith 'out of weakness were made strong,' and 'turned to flight the armies of the aliens' (Hebrews 11:34). So do 'the lame take the prey' (Isaiah 33:23), and the weak become 'as David,' and 'the house of David . . . as the angel of the Lord' (Zechariah 12:8)" (*Thoughts From the Mount of Blessing*, 60–63; see also *Blessings*, 60–63).

Questions to consider

1. How would we feel if Jesus said nothing about the immorality of Las Vegas, but spoke out against our evil thoughts that no one hears? Is it fair for thoughts to be as bad as deeds? Why or why not? Why did Jesus point to thoughts as evil?

2. How is the surrender of the will illustrated here by Jesus? What is only possible if we surrender our will to God?

3. It is a sacrifice to give ourselves to God, but what are we sacrificing and what do we receive in return?

_____

_____

Marriage and Truth   14

This study is based on Matthew 5:31–37; 19:3–8 and
Thoughts From the Mount of Blessing, chapter 3
—see also *Blessings,* chapter 3.

The family of heaven

Looking out on that crowd on the hillside, Jesus could see much misery. The poor, the hungry, the outcasts of society—all followed Him in hope that there was more, that God really did care about them.

In those days, being wealthy and successful was considered a sign of God's pleasure with you. "A person could only be that wealthy if God is blessing them. They must be living the way God wants them to," it was thought. And naturally, the opposite was true as well. "A person that poor, that pathetic, that hopeless must surely have been rejected by God. That person must be a great sinner."

Jesus spent a great deal of time combating this attitude. He went to parties with prostitutes and tax collectors. He told the story of the rich man and Lazarus, where the rich man was not the one God favored. He spoke out in favor of the widow who gave only a mite, instead of the rich man who gave significantly more.

On this morning, Jesus spoke out against another practice that was causing much misery—the divorcing of one's wife. By interpreting the words of Moses in a specific way, the religious leaders had declared that it was acceptable to divorce one's wife for almost any reason. This allowed men to "trade in" their old wives for new ones—younger or richer ones. While technically this allowed the woman to remarry as well, unless they were independently wealthy, it seldom worked that way.

Most often, the woman was left penniless and dependent on extended family, the charity of others, or prostitution to feed herself and her children. These easy divorces destroyed families and left the innocent trapped in a brutal struggle for survival. And the idea that this was acceptable to God, that this was God's plan for families, was an evil Jesus had to speak out against.

In words that must have caused shame among some in the crowd, Jesus spoke out against the easy divorce. On this and other occasions, He pointed people back to the Garden of Eden and God's original plan for marriage. A faithful marriage of love can bless not just the family but the community. A loving family on earth can be our clearest example of the family of heaven.

Jesus also knew that many of the people there on the hillside felt free to take oaths that didn't use God's name. They used these oaths to get away with deception the way "the fine print" of contracts is too often used today. They could deceive another person that way, but couldn't be accused of lying because what they said was "technically" true.

Jesus condemned this kind of oath-taking because it was used as a way to get away with lying and cheating while still pretending to faithfully follow God.

We may not take these kinds of oaths today, but we, too, easily find ourselves gossiping about others, sharing damaging or embarrassing information or suggestions. Far too often we cloak our gossip in the holy garb of "prayer requests." We may sound caring and spiritual when we say, "Pray for them. They're having marriage problems again." Or, "Pray for her. I guess she's still struggling with that bad habit." But we are damaging reputations and lives when we do this. Jesus' teaching to us today would be the same as it was that morning—don't say more than you need to, particularly when speaking about others.

We may not be technically lying when we repeat what we've heard or assume we know the motivation of others' actions. But when our words result in damage to someone's name or reputation, we would find ourselves condemned by Jesus like those He spoke about on the hillside.

Reflect on the story

" 'Is it lawful for a man to put away his wife?' Matthew 19:3.

"Among the Jews a man was permitted to put away his wife for the most trivial offenses, and the woman was then at liberty to marry again. This practice led to great wretchedness and sin. In the Sermon on the Mount Jesus declared plainly that there could be no dissolution of the marriage tie, except for unfaithfulness to the marriage vow. 'Everyone,' He said, 'that putteth away his wife, saving for the cause of fornication, maketh her an adulteress: and whosoever shall marry her when she is put away committeth adultery.' R.V.

"When the Pharisees afterward questioned Him concerning the lawfulness of divorce, Jesus pointed His hearers back to the marriage institution as ordained at creation. 'Because of the hardness of your hearts,' He said, Moses 'suffered you to put away your wives: but from the beginning it was not so.' Matthew 19:8. He referred them to the blessed days of Eden, when God pronounced all things 'very good.' Then marriage and the Sabbath had their origin, twin institutions for the glory of God in the benefit of humanity. Then, as the Creator joined the hands of the holy pair in wedlock, saying, A man shall 'leave his father and his mother, and shall cleave unto his wife: and they shall be one' (Genesis 2:24), He enunciated the law of marriage for all the children of Adam to the close of time. That which the Eternal Father Himself had pronounced good was the law of highest blessing and development for man.

"Like every other one of God's good gifts entrusted to the keeping of humanity, marriage has been perverted by sin; but it is the purpose of the gospel to restore its purity and beauty. In both the Old and the New Testament the marriage relation is employed to represent the tender and sacred union that exists between Christ and His people, the redeemed ones whom He has purchased at the cost of Calvary. 'Fear not,' He says; 'thy Maker is thine husband; the Lord of hosts is His name; and thy Redeemer, the Holy One of Israel.' 'Turn, O backsliding children, saith the Lord; for I am married unto you.' Isaiah 54:4, 5; Jeremiah 3:14. In the 'Song of Songs' we hear the bride's voice saying, 'My Beloved is mine, and I am His.' And He who is to her 'the chiefest among ten thousand,' speaks to His chosen one, 'Thou art all fair, My love; there is no spot in thee.' Song of Solomon 2:16; 5:10; 4:7.

"In later times Paul the apostle, writing to the Ephesian Christians, declares that the Lord has constituted the husband the head of the wife, to be her protector, the house-band, binding the members of the family together, even as Christ is the head of the church and the Saviour of the mystical body. Therefore he says, 'As the church is subject unto Christ, so let the wives be to their own husbands in everything. Husbands, love your wives, even as Christ also loved the church, and gave Himself for it; that He might sanctify and cleanse it with the washing of water by the word, that He might present it to Himself a glorious church, not having spot, or wrinkle, or any such thing; but that it should be holy and without blemish. So ought men to love their wives.' Ephesians 5:24-28.

"The grace of Christ, and this alone, can make this institution what God designed it should be—an agent for the blessing and uplifting of humanity. And thus the families of earth, in their unity and peace and love, may represent the family of heaven.

"Now, as in Christ's day, the condition of society presents a sad comment upon heaven's ideal of this sacred relation. Yet even for those who have found bitterness and disappointment where they had hoped for companionship and joy, the gospel of Christ offers a solace. The patience and gentleness which His Spirit can impart will sweeten the bitter lot. The heart in which Christ dwells will be so filled, so satisfied, with His love that it will not be consumed with longing to attract sympathy and attention to itself. And through the surrender of the soul to God, His wisdom can accomplish what human wisdom fails to do. Through the revelation of His grace, hearts that were once indifferent or estranged may be united in bonds that are firmer and more enduring than those of earth—the golden bonds of a love that will bear the test of trial" (*Thoughts From the Mount of Blessing*, 63–65; see also *Blessings*, (63–65).

Questions to consider

1. What did Jesus teach about marriage in this sermon? Is the world a better place because of marriage? Is the church?

2. How is marriage like the relationship between Christ and His church? What should that mean to us as a church?

3. What would a family on earth look and act like if it is representing the family of heaven?

Reflect on the story

> " 'Never swear an oath' (Matthew 5:34 [NCV]).

"Jesus gives the reason we should not swear: 'Don't swear an oath using the name of heaven, because heaven is God's throne. Don't swear an oath using the name of the earth, because the earth belongs to God. . . . Don't even swear by your own head, because you cannot make one hair on your head become white or black' (Matthew 5:34–36 [NCV]).

"Everything comes from God. We don't have anything that He hasn't given us. Actually, we don't have anything that wasn't bought for us by the blood of Christ. Everything we own comes stamped with a cross, bought with the most precious blood of all. So we have no right to vow or promise anything based on our word as if we owned it.

"The Jews interpreted the third commandment to forbid using God's name profanely, but they felt free to use and take other oaths. From the words of Moses, they knew they could not give false testimony, but they had ways to make sure that what they said was technically correct, even if they knew that it was not exactly truthful. They had no problem lying under oath or misleading others as long as their words were covered by some technical definition of the law.

"Jesus condemned their oath-taking, stating clearly that it was breaking God's law. But Jesus did not forbid the use of a judicial oath, which solemnly calls upon God to witness that what is said is the truth and nothing but the truth. Jesus Himself testified under a judicial oath at His trial before the Jewish court. If He condemned such oath-taking, He would have spoken against it at that time.

"Many people have no problem lying to other people, but they feel much more reluctant to lie to God. Under oath, they feel as if their words are being judged by the One who reads hearts and knows the exact truth. Fear of His judgment encourages them to tell the truth.

"But Christians can testify under oath with no fears. Living their lives each day in the constant presence of God, they have no problem with God being their witness that what is said is the whole truth and nothing but the truth.

"Jesus saw that there was no need for oath-taking. He taught that all that was needed was speaking the exact truth at all times. 'Say only yes if you mean yes, and no if you mean no. If you say more than yes or no, it is from the Evil One' (Matthew 5:37 [NCV]). These words should eliminate the use of meaningless phrases or near-profane expressions. There is no place for false compliments, flattering lies, gross exaggerations, scams, or deceptive trade practices. Jesus' words teach that no one can be called honest who appears to be something he is not or whose words don't tell what is really going on.

"If we followed these words of Jesus, we would stop all of our unkind criticisms of others. How can we comment on another's feelings or motives and be certain that we are speaking the exact truth? Too often, pride, momentary anger, and personal resentment influence the impression we give others. A glance, a word, even the inflection of our voice, can be used to communicate a lie. Even the facts of a situation can be stated in a way that gives a false impression. And whatever is not truth is inspired by Satan.

"Everything that Christians do should be as transparent as the sunlight. Truth is of God. Deception, whatever form it takes, is of Satan. Still, it is not always simple or easy to speak the exact truth. We cannot speak the truth unless we know the truth, but so often preconceived opinions, personal bias, a lack of information, or errors in judgment prevent us from actually understanding the situation accurately. We cannot speak the truth unless our minds are continually guided by the One who is truth.

"Through the words of Paul, Jesus says, 'When you talk, do not say harmful things, but say what people need—words that will help others become stronger. Then what you say will do good to those who listen to you' (Ephesians 4:29 [NCV]). Jesus makes it clear that pointless and unnecessary words, joking, and inappropriate conversations are to be avoided. Our words should not only be truthful, but pure and uplifting.

"Those who are learning to follow Jesus will have no reason to dabble in things that are best done in secret or in darkness. Our words, like our lives, will be simple, honest, and true, for we are training to live happily in the family of heaven" (*Blessings,* 66–68; see also *Thoughts From the Mount of Blessing,* 66–69).

Questions to consider

1. How often are we tempted to speak in ways that are "technically" correct but not entirely truthful? Is it important for a Christian to be truthful all the time?

2. How do we know that Jesus did not forbid taking a judicial oath?

3. How would speaking the truth at all times stop our unkind criticism of others? Would speaking the truth at all times make your life better? How?

4. What is the one way we can know that we always speak the truth?

The Mark of God's Kingdom 15

This study is based on Matthew 5:38–48 and
Thoughts From the Mount of Blessing, chapter 3
—see also *Blessings,* chapter 3.

Turn the other cheek

The quiet peace by the lake was interrupted by distant trumpet blasts. People turned to stare, although they knew what they would see. They saw it all too often—a company of Roman soldiers. With a garrison installed at nearby Capernaum, Roman soldiers were a common sight around the area.

Hatred for the Romans burned especially deep in Galilee, and revolt against them was never far from the surface. Few of the peasants in the crowd had not been forced to carry some equipment for a soldier, bring them food or water, or perform some other degrading task. A number had scars from being beaten down when they objected. They had spent many hours imagining the power to fight back and to drive the Romans out.

When they turned back to look at Jesus, hope shone in their eyes. Could this Man be the Messiah they had waited for? Would He lead them to crush the occupying army and free their land?

But it was a tear that shone in Jesus' eye. He knew they wanted the power to take revenge on their enemies. He knew they wanted Him to lead them into battle. But that was not the way of His kingdom. "If someone slaps you, turn the other cheek," He said quietly. "If a soldier forces you to carry a load for a mile, carry it for two miles."

Most of the people in the crowd could not accept Jesus' words that day. But many followed Him to Jerusalem, where they witnessed Him responding in just that way to His enemies. "Love your enemies," He taught them by His words and deeds.

It is not nationality or religion that qualifies people for the kingdom of heaven. Only one thing proves that we a part of God's family—love. Love for all people. Love even in the face of hate. To be kind in the face of unkindness, to do good without expecting a reward—that is the mark of a true follower of Jesus, a true member of His kingdom.

And that is how we must be perfect. We must reflect His love to all those around us.

In each word of this sermon by the lake, Jesus described what it really means to keep the law—to live in faithful obedience. It means to be like God. It means to reflect the unselfish love that flows out from Him. As Jesus lived to show us His Father, we can live to show the world Jesus.

Reflect on the story

" 'But I tell you, don't stand up against an evil person. If someone slaps
you on the right cheek, turn to him the other cheek also'
(Matthew 5:39 [NCV]).

"The Jewish people were constantly irritated by their contact with the Roman soldiers. Rome had soldiers stationed around Judea and Galilee, and their presence reminded the people that they were a conquered nation. When they heard the loud trumpet blasts and saw the troops assemble around the banner of Rome, their souls boiled with bitterness. Frequent conflicts between the people and the soldiers inflamed the general hatred. Often, a Roman official with a soldier guard, hurrying from one point to another, would seize Jewish peasants working in the fields and force them to carry burdens up a mountainside or give some other service. Roman law and custom permitted this, and any resistance by the peasants led to cruel punishment.

"The people's desire to throw off Roman oppression deepened every day. The spirit of revolt was especially strong among the bold, hardworking people of Galilee. Capernaum, a border town, housed a Roman garrison. While Jesus spoke that day on the hillside, the listening people could see a company of soldiers in the distance, and this brought bitter thoughts to their minds. They looked eagerly at Jesus, hoping He was the Messiah who would drive out the hated Romans.

"Jesus looked into their faces with sadness. He saw that the desire for revenge had stamped its evil mark on them. He knew how much they longed for the power to crush the Roman occupiers. Sadly, He said, 'Don't stand up against an evil person. If someone slaps you on the right cheek, turn to him the other cheek also' (Matthew 5:39 [NCV]).

"These words simply repeated the teaching of the Old Testament. It is true that one of the laws given by Moses said, ' "Eye for eye, tooth for tooth" ' (Leviticus 24:20 [NCV]), but that was for a court of law. No one was justified in taking revenge into their own hands, because God had also said, 'Don't say, "I'll pay you back for the wrong you did." ' 'Don't say, "I'll get even." ' 'If your enemy is hungry, feed him. If he is thirsty, give him a drink' (Proverbs 20:22; 24:29; 25:21 [NCV]).

"Jesus' life on this earth was a demonstration of this principle. He left heaven to bring the bread of life to His enemies, to those who would hate Him. People lied about Him and harassed Him from the cradle to the grave, but He responded only with forgiving love. The prophet Isaiah expressed it this way: 'He was beaten down and punished, but he didn't say a word. He was like a lamb being led to be killed. He was quiet, as a sheep is quiet while its wool is being cut; he never opened his mouth' (Isaiah 53:7 [NCV]). Even on the cross, Jesus prayed for His murderers and gave a message of hope to a dying thief, a story that has been repeated over and over through the ages.

"The Father's presence surrounded Jesus at all times, and nothing happened to Him except those things which were permitted by an infinite love in order to bless the world. This was Jesus' source of comfort, and it can be so for us as well. When we are filled with the spirit of Christ, we live in Him. A blow aimed at us falls instead on the Savior, who surrounds us with His presence. Whatever happens to us comes from Jesus. We don't need to resist evil, because Jesus is our defense. Nothing can touch us without our Lord's permission, and 'in everything God works for the good of those who love him' (Romans 8:28 [NCV]).

" 'If someone wants to sue you in court and take your shirt, let him have your coat also. If someone forces you to go with him one mile, go with him two miles' (Matthew 5:40, 41 [NCV]). Jesus taught His disciples that instead of resisting the demands of those in authority, they should do even more than was asked of them. As far as possible, they should fulfill every request, even if it went beyond what the law required. The Law of Moses expressed great care for the poor. When a poor man had to give his cloak as security for a debt, the creditor was not permitted to go into his house and take it. He had to wait outside for the cloak to be brought to him. And whatever the situation was, the cloak must always be returned at nightfall (see Deuteronomy 24:10–13).

"In Jesus' day, these merciful requirements were largely ignored, but Jesus taught His disciples to submit to the ruling of the court, even if it demanded more than the Law of Moses authorized. Even if the court demanded a part of their clothing, they should give it. They should give their creditor whatever the court authorized him to seize, and be willing to give more if necessary.

"Jesus added, 'If a person asks you for something, give it to him. Don't refuse to give to someone who wants to borrow from you' (Matthew 5:42 [NCV]). Moses had taught the same lesson: 'If there are poor among you . . . do not be selfish or greedy toward them. But give freely to them, and freely lend them whatever they need' (Deuteronomy 15:7, 8 [NCV]). In these words, God isn't teaching us to give indiscriminately to everyone who asks for charity. The text says, 'Freely lend what they need.' But this should be a gift rather than a loan, since we are to 'lend to them without hoping to get anything back' (Luke 6:35 [NCV])" (*Blessings*, 69–72; see also *Thoughts From the Mount of Blessing*, 69–73).

Questions to consider

1. How did Jesus' life demonstrate the principle of "turning the other cheek"?

2. Can we be filled with the spirit of Christ? Can we live in Him? What would that mean in our everyday lives?

3. What would it be like to live giving more than anyone asked of you? Would you be poorer? Busier? Happier?

Reflect on the story

" 'Love your enemies.' Matthew 5:44.

"The Saviour's lesson, 'Resist not him that is evil,' was a hard saying for the revengeful Jews, and they murmured against it among themselves. But Jesus now made a still stronger declaration:

" 'Ye have heard that it hath been said, Thou shalt love thy neighbor, and hate thine enemy. But I say unto you, Love your enemies, bless them that curse you, do good to them that hate you, and pray for them which despitefully use you and persecute you; that ye may be the children of your Father which is in heaven.'

"Such was the spirit of the law which the rabbis had misinterpreted as a cold and rigid code of exactions. They regarded themselves as better than other men, and as entitled to the special favor of God by virtue of their birth as Israelites; but Jesus pointed to the spirit of forgiving love as that which would give evidence that they were actuated by any higher motives than even the publicans and sinners, whom they despised.

"He pointed His hearers to the Ruler of the universe, under the new name, 'Our Father.' He would have them understand how tenderly the heart of God yearned over them. He teaches that God cares for every lost soul; that 'like as a father pitieth his children, so the Lord pitieth them that fear Him.' Psalm 103:13. Such a conception of God was never given to the world by any religion but that of the Bible. Heathenism teaches men to look upon the Supreme Being as an object of fear rather than of love—a malign deity to be appeased by sacrifices, rather than a Father pouring upon His children the gift of His love. Even the people of Israel had become so blinded to the precious teaching of the prophets concerning God that this revelation of His paternal love was as an original subject, a new gift to the world.

"The Jews held that God loved those who served Him,—according to their view, those who fulfilled the requirements of the rabbis,—and that all the rest of the world lay under His frown and curse. Not so, said Jesus; the whole world, the evil and the good, lies in the sunshine of His love. This truth you should have learned from nature itself; for God 'maketh His sun to rise on the evil and on the good, and sendeth rain on the just and on the unjust.'

"It is not because of inherent power that year by year the earth produces her bounties and continues her motion round the sun. The hand of God guides the planets and keeps them in position in their orderly march through the heavens. It is through His power that summer and winter, seedtime and harvest, day and night follow each other in their regular succession. It is by His word that vegetation flourishes, that the leaves appear and the flowers bloom. Every good thing we have, each ray of sunshine and shower of rain, every morsel of food, every moment of life, is a gift of love.

"While we were yet unloving and unlovely in character, 'hateful, and hating one another,' our heavenly Father had mercy on us. 'After that the kindness and love of God our Saviour toward man appeared, not by works of righteousness which we have done, but according to His mercy He saved us.' Titus 3:3-5. His love received, will make us, in like manner, kind and tender, not merely toward those who please us, but to the most faulty and erring and sinful.

"The children of God are those who are partakers of His nature. It is not earthly rank, nor birth, nor nationality, nor religious privilege, which proves that we are members of the family of God; it is love, a love that embraces all humanity. Even sinners whose hearts are not utterly closed to God's Spirit, will respond to kindness; while they may give hate for hate, they will also give love for love. But it is only the Spirit of God that gives love for hatred. To be kind to the unthankful and to the evil, to do good hoping for nothing again, is the insignia of the royalty of heaven, the sure token by which the children of the Highest reveal their high estate" (*Thoughts From the Mount of Blessing*, 73–75; see also *Blessings*, 72–74).

Questions to consider

1. Do we consider ourselves better than other people and entitled to special favors by God because we are Adventists? Do we really believe that God loves the good and the evil equally? How do we show that?

2. What proves that we are members of the family of God? Why is it important to show love to sinners?

Reflect on the story

" 'So you must be perfect, just as your Father in heaven is perfect'
(Matthew 5:48 [NCV]).

"Here, the word *so* implies that the following statement refers to what has been said before. Jesus had been describing God's endless mercy and love. Then He said, 'So you must be perfect.' Because your heavenly Father is kind to those who are unappreciative and to those who are evil, because He has reached down and lifted you up, Jesus says that you can develop a character like His, standing without fault before others—including angels.

"Today, the requirements for eternal life are just the same as they were in Eden—perfect righteousness, harmony with God, and obedience to the principles of His law. The values shown in the Old Testament are the same as those we find in the New Testament. And by God's grace we can live these values. Beneath every law, beneath every command and rule that God gives, lies a powerful promise: God has made a way by which we can become like Him. And He will make this happen for everyone who doesn't interject his or her own will and wishes in the place of God's will.

"God loves us with an astounding love. As our love for Him grows, we will begin to appreciate the length and width and height and depth of this love that can never be measured. As the lovely appeal of Christ begins to be revealed, as we begin to understand the kind of love that He offers us even while we are still sinners, our stubborn hearts are melted. We can now be transformed into children of heaven. God never forces anyone—love is His tool to push sin from the human heart. With love, He changes pride into humility and turns hatred and skepticism into love and faith.

"The Jews had exhausted themselves struggling to reach perfection by their own efforts—and they had failed. Christ had already told them that their kind of righteousness could never enter the kingdom of heaven. Now He points out the kind of character—the kind of righteousness—that everyone who enters heaven will possess. All through this sermon by the lake, Jesus described the outcome of this kind of character. Now, in one sentence, He points out its Source and its nature: be perfect as God is perfect. The law is just a printout of God's character. Look, your heavenly Father is a perfect example of the principles which are the foundation of His government.

"God is love. Like rays of light from the sun, love and light and joy flow out from Him to all His creatures. It is His nature to give. His whole life is about unselfish love. He tells us to be perfect as He is—in the same way. We are to be centers of light and blessing to our little circle, just as God is to the universe. We have no light of our own, but the light of His love shines on us, and we can reflect it. We may be perfect in our circle just as God is perfect in His.

"If we are God's children, we have His nature, so we can't help but be like Him. As a child lives because of his parents, God's children, through the rebirth of the Spirit, live because of Him. All of God—the Father, Son, and Holy Spirit—exists within Jesus, and Jesus lived in human skin. (See Colossians 2:9; 2 Corinthians 4:11.) The life of God within us will create the same character and the same behavior as it did in Jesus. In this way, we will live in harmony with every aspect of God's law. Through love, we can 'be the kind of people the law correctly wants us to be. Now we do not live following our sinful selves, but we live following the Spirit' (Romans 8:4 [NCV])" (*Blessings*, 74–76; see also *Thoughts From the Mount of Blessing*, 76–78).

Questions to consider

1. What was Jesus discussing just before He said, "So you must be perfect"? What does that mean to us?

2. What lies beneath every law, every command that God gives? How can that transform us into the children of heaven?

3. If we are perfect as God is perfect, what will that mean in our circle of family and friends?

Notes

Notes

Notes

Notes

Notes

Notes

Notes

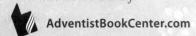
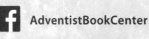
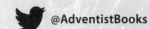

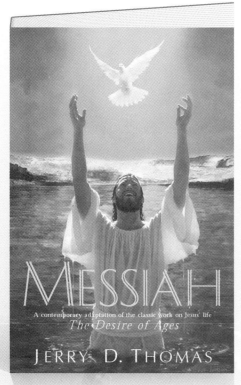

Messiah

"Stepping out of the water, Jesus knelt at the riverbank and prayed. Finally, it was time. Time to begin His public work. Time to begin the fight of His life. . . .

"With eyes that seemed to penetrate to heaven, Jesus poured out His heart . . .

"Only a few in the crowd at the river besides John saw the heavenly miracle. But a sense of a divine presence settled on the people and they stood silently watching Jesus. The light of heaven surrounded Him and His face glowed like no man they had ever seen. A voice from heaven said, 'This is my Son, whom I love, and I am very pleased with him.' "

On the day that sin and suffering entered this world, a promise was given. Someone was coming to make it right. Someone was coming to pay the price. Someone was coming to save us—Jesus, the Savior, the Promised One. The MESSIAH. More than a hundred years ago, Ellen G. White penned *The Desire of Ages,* a classic volume on the life of Jesus. Author Jerry D. Thomas's passion to make this powerful story more accessible to today's reader has given birth to *Messiah*. Like its predecessor, this book lifts up the Man who kept the promise and changed the world. Come and meet the MESSIAH.

Hardcover with dust jacket, 450 pages
ISBN 978-0-8163-1845-2

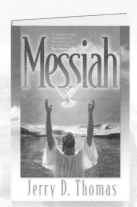

You might also enjoy these editions of *Messiah:*
Condensed sharing edition, saddle-stitched, 64 pages
ISBN 978-0-8163-2334-0

Paperback edition, 448 pages
ISBN 978-0-8163-1978-7

Pocket paperback edition, 603 pages
ISBN 978-0-8163-2132-2

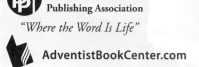

A THOUGHTFUL HOUR

Tracing the Final Footsteps of Jesus

"It would be well for us to spend a thoughtful hour each day in contemplation of the life of Christ. We should take it point by point, and let the imagination grasp each scene, especially the closing ones. As we thus dwell upon His great sacrifice for us, our confidence in Him will be more constant, our love will be quickened, and we shall be more deeply imbued with His spirit." —*The Desire of Ages*, **p. 83**

As precious as the story of Jesus is to each of us, our daily lives keep us so busy that it's hard to find an hour—a thoughtful hour—for reading and studying the Gospel accounts of His life.

That's why this book exists. It is designed to make that thoughtful hour easier, to give a little structure and focus to a study of the life of Christ. Whether you work through the pages as part of a study group or on your own, you will find a fresh look at the gospel story. The questions can be answered as part of a discussion or in your own heart as you read in thoughtful consideration.

Paperback, 96 pages
ISBN 978-0-8163-5020-9

"In *A Thoughtful Hour*, Jerry D. Thomas has masterfully captured the essence of the final chapters of *The Desire of Ages* and developed study guides to accompany his devotional thoughts. Looking to Jesus on the cross, we are changed. This is why I am so enthusiastic about *A Thoughtful Hour*. As you meditate on the life of Christ and consider its closing scenes, your own life will be transformed. It will lead you into an encounter with Jesus that is beyond what you can imagine."
—Mark A. Finley

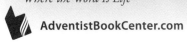